TANGO
ON THE
MAIN

TANGO
ON THE
MAIN

JOE
FIORITO

NUAGE
EDITIONS

1st printing June 1996
2nd printing October 1996

Cover design by Doowah Design.
Photo of Joe Fiorito by Sharon Musgrove.
Front cover photo by David Blanchard.

Acknowledgements
These essays originally appeared in *The Montreal Gazette* 1994-95.
I am indebted to those whose stories I have observed and recorded.
Thanks to Matt Radz and Mark Abley at *The Montreal Gazette* for their editorial assistance, their support and their friendship.

Published with the assistance of The Canada Council and the Quebec Minister of Culture.
Printed and bound in Canada by Veilleux Impression à Demande.

Dépôt légal, Bibliothèque nationale du Québec and the National Library of Canada.

Canadian Cataloguing in Publication Data

Fiorito, Joe, 1948–
    Tango on the Main

Columns previously published in the Montreal Gazette.
ISBN 0-921833-46-6

    I. Title

FC2947.25.F56 1996   C814' .54   C96-900532-6
F1054.5.M853F56 1996

Nuage Editions, P.O. Box 8, Station E
Montréal, Québec, H2T 3A5

For Susan

CONTENTS

APRIL IS THE CRUELLEST MONTH
IN THE GARDENS OF THE PLATEAU

The lawn in front of my house is a tiny green square, a postage stamp of grass placed neatly in front of my address. It is the same for all of us, up and down the rue Christophe Colomb—little philatelic lawns in front of big row houses.

The houses are silent and eloquent as sealed envelopes, waiting at the end of the day for us to open them.

In front of one of these houses, a block away and a world apart, is an ornamental garden, a delicate stamp on a letter from Japan.

Where the rest of us have a patch of grass, here there are two dozen grey and weathered stones, each precisely and randomly placed, each covered with thick green moss.

The stones are the size of the mountains you see in a dream. There are single plants set in their midst. There are one or two dwarf bushes, forests if you squint at them. There is a single tree, clipped so its branches overflow, as if it were a fountain of itself.

One of the bushes keeps its berries all winter long. The berries are red as summer apples. Red as the lights of a Christmas tree. Red as drops of blood.

At the moment the garden lies limp, caught between seasons. It is too soon to breed lilacs—or blood-coloured berries—out of the dead land in Montreal. But it is not too soon for the spring rain to stir dull roots.

The couple who own this garden are middle-class. They are short, not especially stylish people, perhaps a little overweight. They are not old, really, but they are old enough to have retired early.

They have thick hands. They don't say much. They've reached a time in their lives when there is no need to talk, although there is much that is said between them without words.

In the summer he sits on the porch, looking down on his little Japan. He smokes his cigar and reads the papers. He watches while she trims and prunes their tiny front-yard nation with a pair of scissors.

He is a man whose face tells most when it tells the least. I've seen him glance at her through the smoke of his cigar. She bends carefully, snipping a leaf at a time. Her legs are spread for balance. She's a big woman through the hips.

I've seen him stare at her while smoke from his cigar drifts over the tops of the tiny, moss-covered mountains.

Once, on my way home from work, I stopped to say hello, to tell them how much I admired their garden. It was a small act of courage, considering the pitiful state of my French.

"You have a beautiful garden," I said.

I told them it gave me pleasure to see it every day. I told them it looked wonderful even in the winter. She stopped what she was doing, and brushed off her hands, and went inside.

I asked the man if he liked to garden. He seemed amused by my question, almost as amused as he was by my accent.

"My wife does all the work," he said.

I plunged ahead and mentioned a garden I'd read about in the novel *Wind and Stone* by the Japanese writer Masaaki Tachihara.

I told him how, in the novel, a woman was seduced by a gardener without him ever touching her, how the stones he placed and the bushes he planted seemed to speak to the woman with his voice as the seasons changed.

I told him how the flowers he'd planted seduced her.

I remembered a passage from the novel:

"Camellias do not last very long, and when it seemed the red had disappeared from one place in the hedge, blossoms would appear in another location the following morning....one day she had the feeling that the garden had seen her naked, and had violated her."

I didn't attempt a translation of that. I said I thought perhaps the garden was a message meant for him, a message from his wife.

The man looked at me as if I'd lost my mind.

He rustled his newspaper, and cocked his head, pretending he'd heard her say something from somewhere deep inside the house.

We haven't spoken since.

I think they may have gone away for the winter, although I don't think they went to Japan. I think they went to Florida.

The days are getting warmer, although it is still too cold to sit outside with the papers, to linger on the porch in the evening and read the mail.

But spring is here. The couple with the postage-stamp Japan will be home soon. And inside all our houses, April mixes memory and desire.

THE DAY THE ENGLISH LANGUAGE
FELL FROM THE SKY

Not long after I arrived in Montreal, I enrolled in one of those half-and-half language classes for English speakers who want to learn French, and French speakers who want to learn English.

The talk was predictable, chaotic and good-humoured. We stumbled over the movies we'd seen, the food we liked to eat, the shows we watched on television.

One night an elderly francophone man joined my group. He was tall and slender, with courtly manners. He wore a jacket and tie. He seemed formal and slightly sad, the way older people sometimes do.

He also seemed to think we anglos were exotic. Over the course of several evenings, the reason for this became clear. He began to tell me a magical story, and in the manner of the class, he told me bits of it in French and bits of it in English.

As closely as I remember, here is what he said:

I was born more than seventy years ago, and I grew up on a farm. My father was strong and good, although he didn't say very much. He worked very hard in the fields. I thought my mother was the most beautiful woman in the world. We lived on the shores of the St. Lawrence, a long way from Montreal.

One day, when my father had gone into town with the wagon, I happened to be playing in the yard. I heard a noise in the sky. I looked up to see what it could be. It was an airplane, and it seemed to be headed towards our farm.

I had never seen an airplane before, but I knew there were such things. I ran towards the house to tell my mother. She stood in the doorway of the kitchen, watching the sky and drying her hands on her apron.

The plane looked like a big bird. It made a huge noise. It was much louder than the cars which sometimes raced down the road beside our farm.

The plane began to fly in small circles, as if it were going to land. Maman was quiet. She stood with her hands on her hips. I was afraid the plane would crash, but it came to earth safely at the edge of the far field.

Maman and I watched as the airman climbed out. He began to walk towards us. He was walking slowly over my father's field. I was very much afraid. He might have been a god or a devil for all I knew.

He was wearing leather gloves and a leather jacket. He had a pair of goggles pushed up on his forehead, and he wore a pair of knee-high boots. He was smiling. He was a handsome man with good white teeth.

I stood beside maman, and held onto her skirt. My heart was pounding. The strange pilot began to speak in a language I could not understand.

I thought he must be speaking English, even though I had never heard that language before. We spoke only French in our home. The pilot smiled at my mother and pointed to his airplane in the field.

What happened next filled me with wonder.

Maman began to speak English to the stranger who had fallen from the sky. Until that very moment, she had spoken nothing but French to me and my father. Now suddenly, here she was speaking English!

How could this be?

Had the English language fallen from the sky and landed in my mother's mouth? Had the strange airman, with some magical device, given her the power to understand the words he spoke?

I wondered what my father would think about this. Why hadn't I received this gift of tongues? Why couldn't I understand what the strange pilot said? Maman invited him into the kitchen and began to make tea. He wiped off his boots in the doorway and sat down at the table.

What would papa say?

I waited outside in the yard with the chickens. I could hear the strange sounds of the English language coming from the kitchen. I could see the shiny boots of the magical pilot through the open kitchen door.

Eventually my father came home with his wagon and horses. My mother told him what had happened. She spoke to him in French, thank God.

Father shook hands with the stranger, and had a cup of tea. Then he helped the pilot haul the plane to solid ground and he gave the man some gasoline.

The pilot shook hands with my father again, and climbed inside his plane. It started with a roar, wobbled off down the field and then rose above the trees. It circled once around the house, dipped its wing, and flew away. I stood in the yard and waved goodbye. The English-speaking airman disappeared forever.

Later, as we sat down for supper, I asked how it was that maman had suddenly been able to speak English.

Maman laughed. She said that when she was young, she had gone to work in the cotton mills of New England. She had learned English as a factory girl in Vermont, before she met papa. There'd been no reason to speak the language again, until the day the airman landed in our field.

With that, the story ended and seventy years fell away. But the old man's eyes remained filled with wonder, as if he were still a boy, as if the English language had just fallen from the sky and landed in his mother's mouth.

THE CHINESE MEN WHO OUTLIVED GUY FAVREAU

The story of the Chinese men begins with a yellow ambulance and a Chinese woman in the towers of the Complexe Guy Favreau.

The woman is wearing a hot pink baseball cap. It is early in the morning. She is lying on her back. She is belted to a stretcher. Two men are wheeling her away.

The sound of her silk skirt has stopped. On the marble pavement dust grows. Her empty room is cold and still. Fallen leaves are piled against the doors. Longing for that lovely lady, how can I bring my aching heart to rest? [1]

This is not an auspicious start. I do not want to tell you the story of an old Chinese woman dying on a stretcher.

I want to tell you about the Chinese men.

They sit and smoke all day on benches in the lower level of the Complexe Guy Favreau. They squint through the smoke. They see everything and nothing. They are silent for a time. And then they start to laugh again, to wave their hands and talk.

Life goes on.

The Chinese men gather here every morning to tell each other stories, to eat leftover noodles from home, to read the *Sing Tao Daily* paper, to close their eyes and nap. They used to meet upstairs, at street level.

As recently as last fall, they used to sit by the windows and watch the street and let the sun bake their bones. And then the government cracked down on smoking and the old men had to move downstairs.

Now the smoke from all their cigarettes rises through the atrium in the centre of the building. The blue smoke is like incense offered to the grandeur of Favreau. Carved in the stone pedestal which supports the bust of Monsieur Favreau are the words "La tolerance est la condition de la dignité même des hommes et leurs cultures."

Tolerance.

As long as you smoke downstairs.

Favreau was a former federal minister of immigration. He died nearly thirty years ago of a busted career and a broken heart. Some thought the complex built to bear his name was a square block of intolerance which would break the heart of the Chinese quarter—it was too big, it took up too much room, its brick and glass towers were the last straw.

Here was a brutal irony—a building named for a minister of immigration would destroy an immigrant neighbourhood.

But old Chinese men are no strangers to irony.

Every day for the past ten years, they have come trickling back into the building. They are drops of water that wear away the stone. They have taken over the building with their cigarettes and their laughter.

Their laughter is a language unto itself. As if to say, We're not going anywhere, ha ha ha. We're not in any hurry. There are more of us where we came from, ha ha ha.

Immigration officials and other federal bureaucrats scurry through this laughter for a quick fag of their own. The bureaucrats wear suits with padded shoulders. They carry padded envelopes. They ignore the Chinese men.

The Chinese men wear padded parkas and padded ear-flap caps. They ignore the bureaucrats. It is a waiting game, and I know who I'm betting on.

One of these old men sits on a bench outside the Ruby Sandy Coiffure Unisexe. The hours of the shop are posted in Chinese—water, wearing away stone.

The old man watches women's haircuts through the window. The scene at Ruby Sandy's is as good as any television, except it's cheaper and it's live, and the woman cutting hair is wearing a red dress.

Further down the corridor, another old man stops and stares at a trio of school-aged kids. The old man is tiny and commanding as an emperor. His hands are clasped behind his back. He stares.

The kids are dressed in baggies. They ignore him, but they know they're being watched. They walk over to the pay phones, make a call, and check the phones for change. They go away.

The old men buy their daily papers at the Star Bookstore on La Gauchetière. If they're old men from Taiwan, they read the *World*

Journal. If they're old men from Hong Kong, they read the *Sing Tao Daily.* Today they learn that Canada won't hand out dual citizenships to Quebeckers if Quebec secedes.

I don't know what they make of that.

I cannot speak Chinese.

A maintenance man comes by to sweep up butts. The old men pay no mind. They do not seem to see the point. They have outlived emperors and warlords. They have outlived Mao and Deng. At the end of the day, they'll outlive the Complexe Guy Favreau.

Will they outlive the woman in the hot pink baseball cap?

A year ago inside this door, her pretty face, the peach flowers each to each reflected pink. Pretty Face! Where is she now? Still the peach flowers, crinkling in spring wind. [2]

She should be okay, says a white-shirted commissionaire. She has diabetes. She didn't have a heart attack. And what of the old Chinese men?

They'll be back tomorrow.

[1] From *One Hundred and Seventy Chinese Poems*, translated by Arthur Waley (Jonathan Cape).

[2] From "Old Friend from Far Away," *150 Chinese Poems from the Great Dynasties* (North Point Press).

NO HISSING OF SUMMER LAWNS IN THE PLATEAU

Anyone would think my neighbour was a monk.

His hair is white, and makes a close-trimmed fringe around his scalp. He keeps his own counsel. His gaze is simple and direct.

He wears short-sleeved rayon shirts and dark-green cotton work pants, as if he were a brother on vacation with the folks at home. His arms are strong and brown from working hard outdoors.

He doesn't go out with women, as far as I know. He spends most of his time in the neighbourhood, cutting grass, raking leaves, looking after things. He needs the pocket money. His needs are simple.

He's retarded.

He has the appearance of a sixty-year-old man and the demeanour of a six-year-old boy, if you happen to live in a neighbourhood where the six-year-old boys are five-foot ten and weigh two hundred pounds.

Jean-Paul lives next door with Monsieur and Madame L. It is a useful arrangement—Jean-Paul isn't stuck in an institution, Monsieur and Madame get a small allowance for his board, and they get some help around the house.

They need the help. Monsieur can't work as hard as he used to after the trouble with his heart and Madame needs help from time to time with a bag of groceries or a basket of laundry. The three of them are comfortable with each other.

When I first moved into the neighbourhood, my landlord told me Jean-Paul would do the lawn, and from the tone of his voice I understood there would be no argument. It was a neighbourhood thing, almost a part of the lease.

Jean-Paul and I get along fine, although from our first meeting, it wasn't certain that we would.

I was unpacking boxes of books when the doorbell rang. I knew the man at the door would be Jean-Paul. I knew by the electric mower idling on the lawn, and I knew by the careful way he'd coiled the extension cord.

I expected our first meeting to be about as complicated as kindergarten. Then Jean-Paul pointed to the lawn and spoke some words I couldn't understand. His voice was thick, made thicker by his Plateau accent.

I smiled and said in my best language-school French that I didn't understand. I was proud of that sentence. I'd worked hard on it, and I was happy to have the chance to try it out on somebody who wouldn't turn his nose up at my accent.

Instead, he stared at me as if I was playing a trick.

It was a trick he clearly didn't like. It was too hot and he was working too hard to have patience with tricks. He stared at me as if to say he had no time for foolishness from people who were smart.

Again he asked a question.

I had no idea what he said, and I could feel his impatience rising. I said, more carefully now, that I didn't really speak French. I said it perfectly. I had the accent down. I've had lots of practise with that sentence.

I could see him thinking. "If this guy can't speak French, then how come he can tell me that he can't speak French? His French sounds fine to me. Who's he trying to kid? It better not be me. "

I could see that in his eyes.

His mouth set hard and his eyes grew narrower. Jean-Paul is very strong. He has thick and muscular arms, and he waved them as he talked. He made a fist and jerked his thumb at the lawn. It was a big fist, with a strong thumb. I didn't know what to say.

Jean-Paul stopped looking at the lawn and looked at me. I'd exhausted my vocabulary. His gaze was getting harder. There was a trace of sweat along his upper lip, He wiped it off, and my mind raced.

We were on the cusp of one of those irretrievable moments when anything could have happened, and whatever that might be, there was a good chance it wouldn't be pleasant. There would be no going back.

And then the penny dropped.

He wanted a rake.

He'd finished cutting the lawn, he wanted to rake the grass. It was so simple that had to be it, it couldn't be anything else. "Wait for me right here," I said in perfect, if panicky, French. I raced downstairs to get the rake.

I knew I was right. I hoped I was right. I wondered what would happen if I was wrong. I remembered the kitten in *The Grapes of Wrath*.

He grasped the rake.

He looked at me as if to say "If you can't speak any French, how did you know I wanted the rake?"

I couldn't tell him how I knew. I still don't know, unless it is that panic plays a significant role in the sudden acquisition of language.

Jean-Paul cut the last lawns of the summer a couple of weeks ago. These days he's raking yards and bagging leaves. These days, I know what he wants when he bangs on my door. He taught me how to say it.

The word for rake is râteau.

Kindergarten, indeed.

THE LUCK OF THE DRAW HAD
NOTHING TO DO WITH CHRISTMAS

My father delivered mail for a living, and I can tell you this about mailmen: they hate the cold as much as they hate the mail. Christmas, with its icy wind and slippery walks and Christmas cards, is a physical ordeal for anyone with a heavy sack.

Still, my old man enjoyed the usual postman's consolations. Every night when he came home from work, shivering and cold to the bone, he'd have a mailbag full of presents from the people on his route.

There were small boxes of chocolates and tins of cigarettes. There were cigars in silver tubes, and mickeys of brandy or rum, clumsily wrapped with red ribbons and green paper. When he came home and handed them to my mother, these little luxuries were still cold from the outdoors.

And in the bottom of his mailbag, there were piles of Christmas cards with money tucked inside, singles and twos and fives. When I was young, I got to dig around inside the bag when he came home. I loved to separate the money from the cards. I loved the soft colours and the strangely metallic smell of the bills.

The money was important.

There never was enough. Between the two of them, my parents worked three jobs. In spite of that, money was one of the tensions in the marriage. There was whispered talk every month, and sometimes the talk was louder than a whisper.

There simply wasn't enough. I was uncomfortable knowing that my parents depended on Christmas tips, and that each year they hoped for a generous season.

I knew, even at the age of ten, that if you live on hope, you starve. Still, like all children, my brothers and I were full of hope at Christmas. We hoped we wouldn't get soft presents, shirts or pants or socks. We hoped for the hard presents, leather footballs and skates and boxes with popular toys.

Often we didn't get the toy we wanted, but we'd get something more affordable and almost exactly like it. Something almost like it, as anyone knows who was a child in a family that didn't have much money, or whose children clamour now for something out of reach, is not the same thing. So we learned early to feign surprise and mask our disappointment, useful skills at any age.

In those days, when I was young, the businessmen in our part of town held a draw on Christmas Eve. It was a big draw for a lot of money, and every year we bought a ticket. You had to show up with your ticket at the draw to win, but on Christmas Eve the year I was ten, my old man came home tired and too cold from work to go out again.

The weather was too bitter for my mother to walk downtown, my older brother was beneath such errands by that time, and my little brothers were too young.

"Take the tickets to the draw, Joe," said my dad. "You look lucky. Win us all some money." I wanted to win that money more than anything. I wanted to see my parents laughing with big green fistfuls of it.

And so I got dressed in my heavy coat and I put on my rubber boots, and I stuck the ticket in my mitt, where I knew I wouldn't lose it. I tried feeling lucky as I left the house.

Down the block, I turned right at the school and walked past the church and the grocery store. There was nobody on the street. It was too cold and too dark outside, in spite of all the houses strung with lights, and the Christmas trees blinking in all the windows.

When I got downtown, there was a small crowd shivering around a flatbed truck in the middle of the street. The mayor and some local merchants stood on the truck, covering their ears and blowing on their hands and stamping their feet to keep warm.

They were waiting for everyone to show up, so they could get back to their families. We were getting restless, too. There was muttering, and our breath rose in little white clouds above the muttering until somebody yelled something from the back of the crowd about getting the damn thing done.

The mayor took off his pearl-grey gloves and made a joke about the cold. He wore a grey homburg and a black wool top-coat with a velvet collar. The scarf around his throat was white, immaculate and silk.

None of us with tickets were as well or warmly dressed.

But I saw some men smiling broadly and laughing a little too loud at the mayor's joke about the cold. "That Ernie," they said. "He's a regular guy, isn't he?"

I didn't understand why anyone would toady to this man who never worked with his hands except to flip the pages of an actuarial table or add up lists of sums. He was the mayor and an insurance man and that was all. He hadn't worked outside all day in the cold. He didn't work as hard as my old man.

The leader of the local merchants spun the drum.

The drum spun slowly and then faster, and I could hear the paper tickets sliding and tumbling inside. My feet tingled with the cold, and I could feel the wind as it slipped beneath the collar of my coat. All the warmth in me had gathered in my hand, protecting the lucky number.

And then the drum stopped spinning and the mayor stuck his hand in, and I heard the number that was drawn, and I didn't have to look.

On the way back, all I could think about was the mayor's silk scarf and his grey gloves, and my neighbours standing in the cold. The draw had been a long shot. It was a long walk home.

But when I got in the door and stamped my boots, the house was just as festive as it had been when I left, with strings of Christmas cards and paper bells and streamers in the living room. The tree with its bright glass decorations was still blinking near the window, and even if some of them were soft, the presents underneath it were piled high.

Chance had nothing to do with that.

PASTEL NAZIS

Moise Peer is a tiny man with piercing eyes and a tight smile which admits no humour. He is sitting by himself at a table in the courtyard of the World Trade Centre, looking lost in the soft light.

Mr. Peer is a survivor of the Holocaust.

He sits with his hands in his lap. In front of him are several piles of *UBB: Unforgettable Bergen-Belsen,* the book he wrote a year and a half ago about his experiences as a French child in the German death camp.

Behind him there are several panels of gruesome Holocaust photos.

Every week, Peer visits a different Montreal mall with his book and his display. Last week, he was in the Galeries de Terrebonne. The week before that, he was in a mall in Laval. Next week, he'll be at the Rockland Centre.

Peer was nine years old when he was arrested in France in 1942. He was a little French Jew with barn-door ears, happy and eager to please. He survived three years in the camp.

The pictures in his display have been peculiarly hand-tinted. They show skeletal, pastel Jews and lime-green Nazis, colourful maps of the death camps, German military plans, contemporary propaganda cartoons, the partial texts of old news reports, the testimony of survivors.

Peer coloured the pictures himself with felt markers, to highlight where they have faded. The effect is fresh and gruesome.

There is a picture of two Russian Jews with orange hair, hanging by the neck from pink ropes. A picture of Nazi propagandist Joseph Goebbels with an orange hand, a pink tie and a yellow swastika. A picture of a skinny Jewish man with yellow legs, and a picture of a shoeless Jewish child with yellow feet.

There is a picture of Heinrich Himmler with an orange nose and a green hat. Himmler is talking with Max Faust, chief engineer for

I.G. Farben. Faust has orange piping on his suit, a yellow hat, an orange nose.

Murderers as clowns.

Mr. Peer watches people come and go all day.

Some of the passers-by look once at his display, and look away quickly in disgust. Some stop and look but they will not look closely, as if the photos might come to life.

Some stare closely, intently, seeking the tiniest detail, searching for a clue to the horrors of the human heart. And some don't look at all; they swing their briefcases jauntily, their high heels ticking like clocks on the brick-tiled floor.

Peer pulls a sweet bun from a plastic bag. "My snack for five o'clock tea." How often does he do this? "Forty weeks a year." Why does he do it? "Because I want to." His eyes dart quickly from side to side. He laughs, but it is an empty laugh. He knows there is nothing funny about what he is doing, and nothing funny about what was done to him. His mother, his aunt and his grandmother died in Auschwitz.

He wants people to remember.

How many books has he sold today? "Six or seven." Did he have to pay to set up his display? "You know somebody who gets something for nothing?" Yes, but how much did he pay? He smiles, and a shrug steals the humour from his face.

Occasionally, Peer engages a passerby in conversation.

Occasionally he sells a book.

I watch a man frown at a photo of Adolph Hitler signing a treaty. Hitler is bent over the treaty, pen in hand. He has yellow hair, green lapels and an orange hand. The colours make him seem more evil.

As if that were possible.

The man approaches Mr. Peer and asks bluntly, "Why should I buy this book? How is it different from the others I've read?" Mr. Peer peers at his questioner. He answers quickly, as if he might run out of time. "This is the first book about Bergen-Belsen. It is the first book about French children deported to Germany..."

"How different from the experience of the Polish?" interrupts the man. Peer says, "Most books about the Holocaust are about Central European Jews. I am a French Jew, a child of the Holocaust, I am the only one who..."

"Okay, okay, you sold me," says the man.

Moise Peer signs his book. The man asks if anyone ever argues that the Holocaust did not happen. Peer purses his lips and looks away in disgust. "One in thousands, maybe."

Peer printed the book himself. He made four thousand copies, half of them in French and half in English. How many has he sold? "I don't like to say. I might give a wrong number." How long will it take for him to sell out? "The rest of this year and all of the next."

What does he do when he's not selling books? "I'm semi-retired. I am selling some of my land, but to tell you the truth, nothing sells now. I haven't sold any land for a year. Who buys land to pay taxes?"

The book costs twenty bucks. Peer opens one for me and signs his name. Behind his head are photos of pastel Nazis, pink Hitlers, storm troopers in lime-green helmets, Jews with yellow feet.

He adds the date and this inscription:

"How can we forget?"

FRIENDS BREAK BREAD TOGETHER
AND TALK ABOUT INTOLERANCE

The day after the referendum, some friends came over for dinner. Not to celebrate, so much as to breathe a sigh of relief following the narrow failure of the politics of brinkmanship. It was not long before the stories came tumbling out.

One man said his Italian mother met a neighbour on the street on voting day. The neighbour, a francophone, greeted the Italian woman and said, "After we win, we're coming for your house." A jest, obviously, but also a slap in the face, and the striking of a fearful chord.

The Italian woman was having none of it—she knows the tunes that fascists sing, she's heard the music of their hard guitars. Her reply was swift and measured. "I'll burn my house down before anyone can take it away from me," she said.

We ate, we drank. We talked.

Another story: the morning after the ballots were counted, Susan went to the gym to work off some of the tension. Nobody was talking politics at the gym—nobody talks much there anyway, because of the loud music—but on this of all mornings, she felt a misplaced word might have broken the very thin ice into very hard shards.

When the instructor asked the class to pair off, Susan, an anglophone, found herself face to face with a francophone partner. The instructor asked the women to grasp each other's hands for balance, and then to raise their opposite legs to the side—some kind of stretching exercise.

The two women faced each other in perilous balance, each standing on one leg, each steadying the other. Susan didn't say a word, for fear of identifying herself by her accent. For fear of toppling a delicate balance.

The evening wore on. Wine flowed. Tongues loosened. We wondered what Preston Manning could possibly have been thinking when, at a defining moment in the life of the nation, he reached back into history and made reference to the awakening of a sleeping tiger—words first spoken by General Yamamoto, after the attack on Pearl Harbour.

Huh?

He could have cited Laurier: "Canada has been the inspiration of my life. I have had before me as a pillar of fire by night and a pillar of cloud by day a policy of true Canadianism, of moderation, of conciliation."

He could have cited Bruce Hutchison: "The Canadian breed has sometimes missed its way. It has never failed a single decisive test when the alternatives were clear. If you can clarify the present alternatives, the right choice will be made again. Whatever else it may lack, the nation is rich in sanity."

He could even have cited Eugène Cloutier: "At certain hours, there is no solution: half the human race scares you, and the other half bores you."

But he chose General Yamamoto, the imperialist, the sneak attacker. So much for statesmanship in the modern age. So much for the intellectual depth of the self-styled leader of reform in this country.

The television flipped back and forth, a ping-pong of post-mortems on the French and English news. We watched on, tired, giddy, fascinated. Ethnics all, we knew that Parizeau had not apologized for the ugliness of his remarks the night before, remarks which turned us into scapegoats.

Someone spoke seriously and sadly about emigrating, about wanting to move to a place where "otherness" was not a thing to hide, where being "ethnic" was not a badge of identification; after all, some of the people in the room had relatives who'd been forced to wear badges by thugs whose goal was racial purity.

Later in the evening, out of the corner of my eye, I saw the TV camera enter the bakery where I'd bought that evening's bread. The bakery is near my house. It is locally famous, artisanal, and proudly Quebecois. They make the best bread in the city. The camera was looking for reaction to the results of the referendum.

The woman behind the counter said she did not like the fact that "ethnics come here to enjoy the culture, but they will not help us preserve it"—"us" being the *vieille souche* Quebeckers. "They" being me and my friends.

My stomach soured.

I would like to go back to that bakery now and look that woman in the face. I would like to tell her that I support her culture when I buy her bread, that I support her dream when I pay my taxes. I would like to tell her that I will not beg to belong, no matter how well I am "treated" by her or anyone else.

I would like to tell her that, in a democracy, I am free to live where I choose, free to vote according to my beliefs, whether or not they coincide with hers. I would like to say *ce n'est pas mon rêve,* the creation of a racial state.

I would like to buy a loaf and break it in two and leave it on the counter in front of her. I will not; I've lost my taste for grand gestures. But I won't go there again. I've lost my taste for bread made with a thin crust of intolerance.

·　　·　　·

I got a lot of phone calls as a result of this column. I also got a lot of mail, most of it in support of what I had written. There was some curious negative response. One person, anonymous and clearly agitated, accused me in abusive language of belonging to the Mafia.

There was one more anonymous letter.

It wasn't sent to me.

A woman wrote to the owner of the bakery. She said she, too, wasn't going to buy any more bread. She sent him a copy of my column. She told the baker that the remarks made by his clerk were tribal and intolerant. She said bread is supposed to be a symbol of sharing.

How do I know this?

My baker told me so.

He wrote to me, to say he was filled with sadness. He said he made bread for everyone. He said it was not his dream to live in a racial state, in a Quebec run by demagogues. He suggested it was time for us to be larger than our judgements; he asked if we could meet each other, face to face.

I called him and suggested coffee.

With some nervousness, we agreed on a time and place. We would talk about my column. We would talk about his clerk. We would find out how badly the devil had poisoned the debate.

We met at a working-class coffee shop in our neighbourhood. The baker and I laughed nervously when we shook hands. I wasn't sure what to expect, and neither was he—we were two strangers, thrown against each other in the heat of a peculiar battle.

Slowly and carefully, I told him that many of us "others"— ethnics, anglophones, people who come from away—are frightened by the rhetoric, threatened by the debate, appalled by the lack of imagination coming from our leaders.

He said he, too, was disturbed by the politics of division. He said he was ashamed of what some leaders had said in the hours immediately following the referendum. He said the real problems in society—bread and butter issues, if you will—were being ignored for the sake of nasty political games.

We talked about what we have in common—among other things, he is a baker who writes, and I am a writer who bakes. We seemed on the verge of a beginning, as if we had built one tiny bridge across a sea of misunderstanding.

He showed me something he had written in preparation for our meeting. The gist of it is this: *Life in the city is anonymous and impersonal. Sometimes even a simple "hello" can be a barrier between people. Many of us were hurt by the referendum. How can we break down the wall that politicians have built between us?*

We'd made a start.

But what about the remarks made by his clerk? Could I face her, could she face me? The baker asked if I would come to the bakery the next morning. He asked if I'd like to meet her. He asked if I would help make some of that day's bread.

You bet I would.

Sabine was charming. We smiled and shook hands and rolled our eyes skyward, as if to say how curious all this was. I gave her a package of home-made cookies, and spent a couple of hours making bread.

I worked with big Fabien, who has an angry scar on his forearm from one of the hot pans, with Raymond, the former bicycle courier with the flashing smile and the red beret, and with Sabine, who started it all.

I also worked alongside my new friend, Benoît. He showed me how to knead dough. He told me about his new baby. When I was done, he let me keep my apron and he gave me a loaf of bread.

A simple gesture.

I think if there is going to be a new Quebec, a new Canada, it will be made at this level, face to face and without politics. It will be made with the warmth of friendship and the dignity of work. It will be made in our neighbourhoods, over our back fences. It will be made with little gestures.

Perhaps with a loaf of bread.

ON SUNDAY HE CLIMBS
TO THE TOP OF THE MOUNTAIN

Father Bob Nagy—the name is Hungarian, his friends call him Nudge—rents a small room in the rectory of an east end parish. He lives simply, even for a priest.

The room he rents is furnished with a cot and a desk, a couple of chairs and a computer. One of the chairs holds a pair of his pants and a shirt. There are runners and sandals scattered neatly on the floor. There is a crucifix on the wall above the bed.

On his bookshelves, alongside the usual leather-bound prayerbooks, are some titles you might not expect. *Inner Tennis. Dead Souls. The Divine Comedy.* These days, Father Bob is reading *All the Pretty Horses.*

His is very much a student's room.

Which is apt, in a way—Father Bob is assigned to the Loyola campus of Concordia University. His flock is composed of university students, staff and faculty. Nudge has an intellectual ministry, a ministry of doubt.

His parishioners are people looking for answers in a world with too many fundamental questions. Tucked comfortably among the skeptics and free thinkers, there is also a scattering of elderly single women and shy men who are uncomfortable in any other parish.

Father Bob's is not an easy job.

On Saturdays, he rises early. He puts on his sweatpants and his Birkenstocks. He takes a coffee, reads the papers and chats with his fellow priests in the rectory kitchen. Then he starts work on the homily for Sunday morning.

Father Bob has yet to master his computer fully. He writes his homily in longhand on a lined pad. There was a time when he spoke without the benefit of notes at mass. Until his parishioners suggested that perhaps the homilies went on just a bit too long.

He reports this wistfully.

I detect a scintilla of regret.

When he needs a break from writing the homily, Father Bob carves wood. Among his works is a statue of St. Francis embracing Sister Death. It is a striking piece.

Sister Death is a womanly and seductive skeleton. But the face of the wooden St. Francis resembles the face of the living Nudge. He carved it after a friend died in a climbing accident. Father Bob no longer climbs.

These days he is carving a mahogany frieze. It is destined for the chapel of his church. When finished, it will be rampant with vines and grapes and angels flowing above a crowd of people at worship, and a person in a wheelchair.

I've come to ask about the homily.

This week, it is based on the story of the scribe Ezra, who restored the word of the law to the men and women who had been exiled. On hearing the word after years in the desert, the men and women fell down.

This week, Father Bob will also perform a baptism. He will try to link the baptism to the story of Ezra. I'm curious to know what kind of connection he'll make between the old scribe and the new baby. But the homily isn't finished.

The only way to hear it is to go to mass.

As we speak, a retired priest pedals an exercise bike slowly and steadily in the hall of the rectory. Maybe the way to heaven is heaven, and maybe an old priest can get there on an exercycle. I have no idea.

I haven't been to church in years.

Mass is scheduled for eleven, but it's snowing on Sunday morning. The roads are slick and the congregation is slow to arrive. Father Bob will not be working a full house today.

He prepares for mass by suiting up. He wears a rough white alb with a hood, a green chasuble, and a green-and-gold stole. His garments were made by his parishioners. Strapped around his waist is the battery pack for a Radio Shack microphone.

Mass begins with prayers and song.

This crowd may be freethinkers, but they know the call and response of the modern Catholic church. I am a stranger to my pew, and I don't recognize any of the tunes, but I sneak in a sign of the cross whenever it seems appropriate.

Father Bob begins to read his longhand homily.

He wonders if this infant will hear the word of the law the way the exiles did. He observes that few children go to church today. He calls on us to embrace our differences for the sake of the baby. The infant is the son of former parishioners who now live in the States. They have returned to the Loyola chapel on this day because of Father Bob.

Suddenly, the homily turns a sharp corner.

Father Bob refers to the disgrace of the First Airborne. He says we must embrace our vulnerability or we will not change a single thing in the world. We are, says Father Bob, a product of our age. We want control because we are afraid.

Control does not allow, he says, for the suddenness of God.

He tells the parents to bring the infant to the baptismal font. He gathers all the children in the congregation around him and asks if they will help. The children suck their thumbs and look for their mothers. One of the children is given a towel to hold, another one holds a book.

Father Bob makes the sign of the cross on the baby's forehead. It sneezes. Someone in the congregation says, "Bless you!" There is a flicker, a suddenness of laughter in the church.

After several anointings and the ritual pouring of water, baby Aaron is given his name, and the children are given lit candles. Father Bob walks down the aisle with Aaron in his arms. He is followed by the parents and the godparents, and the children with their candles.

The sound of a flute soars over the applause.

When mass continues, Father Bob asks if there are special prayers. A young man asks us to pray for a colleague who has lost his eyesight as a complication of AIDS. A woman asks us to pray for all the mothers. Another woman quickly asks us to pray for all the fathers. Everybody smiles, as if men need special prayers.

When the bread and wine have been transformed—the bread has been made by a member of the parish, the wine is Portuguese, and ordered by the church in bulk—Nudge calls on us to greet each other.

Before I can prepare myself, people I don't know are smiling and shaking my hand. They look me in the eye and say, "I wish you peace!"

This will surprise no one who has been in a Catholic church recently. But I have not, and I am utterly disoriented. I smile in spite of myself and sputter, "Peace to you, too!" It is oddly refreshing, both innocent and communal.

Mass draws to a close, and Father Bob reminds his flock that there is still time to sign up for the winter retreat. The freethinkers go home in the snow.

The priesthood is not an easy business.

The competition is significant. There are Sunday morning cartoons. There is the impediment of the weather, and the simple need to sleep late between warm sheets on a cold morning.

Who needs God?

Father Bob nudges us towards the answer.

THE TREVOR WILLIAMS ALL-STAR BASKETBALL CAMP

There's a black kid sleeping on a park bench in the still air near the gym doors of the Polyvalente St. Henri. It's early in the morning, so hot your shirt is damp before you hit the sidewalk.

The kid is waiting for the Trevor Williams All-Star Basketball Camp to start. He's been sleeping on the bench since eight. Camp doesn't start until ten. That tells you something about the kid, maybe more than you wanted to know.

And it tells you a thing or two about Trevor Williams—here's a guy who learned to play basketball in Little Burgundy, who stole the ball from Scottie Pippin at the last Olympics, a guy who could be making a pile of money in an air-conditioned gym in Europe if he wanted to; instead he's teaching hoops to ghetto kids on a hot day in an inner-city sweatbox.

The kids look up to him for it. They come from all over town to be here. All kinds of kids. Black kids and white kids, kids with hard asses from hard families. Kids like the sleepy little bench player.

There are maybe fifty of them in the gym today. They are a festival of gangly. Their names are Moustafa and Shawn, Jamal and Kristal and Kayo. Their shoes look like black lunch pails on their feet. They wear t-shirts that scream "Razorbacks," "Italia World Cup" and "Plattsburgh State."

Plattsburgh State?

By ten-fifteen, their tongues are hanging out. Trevor and his instructors have got them hopping up and down, balancing basketballs over their heads. The gym reeks of fresh sweat, old sneakers and the memory of floor wax.

You can't make a living doing this.

Trevor isn't in it for the money. What's in it for him and his instructors? Some weeks, maybe $150. Some weeks nothing, depending on registration. Why do they do it? They're all from

Little Burgundy, they all love hoops, they want to give these kids a chance. You could say, in the summer heat, that they're pouring water on their roots.

It's a big job. Trevor can't do it on his own. He begs and borrows what he needs. He calls favours, he gets a bit of help from Tommy Kane. No, he gets a lot of help from Tommy Kane. He also gets help from Bob White.

If you know anything about black kids in this town, you know about Bob White. Bob's a teacher and a preacher of the virtues of education, he's a hustler and a muscler of athletic scholarships for the kids of Little Burgundy.

Bob watches me watch the kids in the gym, who by now are bouncing balls between their legs. The balls are a tam-tam of noise on the hardwood floor.

Trevor works the kids, Bob works me. Why can't these kids get a gym in Little Burgundy? What would these kids be doing if they weren't at basketball camp? Who's gonna help them if we don't? Bob White has a hundred questions, but they're all the same question. He knows what the answer is.

So do I, so do you.

"Hey, Justin," calls Trevor, "where were you yesterday?" Justin is a little kid with a porridge bowl haircut. He shakes his sleepy head and grins.

Trevor is one of the answers.

The sessions cost $75 a week. Not all of these kids pay full fare. Some pay what they're able to pay, and sometimes another parent kicks in a little extra money, which is another kind of answer.

Trevor gathers the kids under a basket and says they can't take a water break until somebody hits two free throws in a row. The kids line up thirsty and focussed. Trevor says, "A kid has to learn to handle pressure; it's going to help him later in life." It takes five kids before someone hits two in a row.

Trevor sucks back some Gatorade, and huddles with his instructors. Bob says, "This is real multiculturalism, right here. You got dreads playing yarmulkes. It's like the keyboard on the piano. You get music from black and white keys."

At lunchtime, the instructors pass around a cardboard box full of egg salad on white, a gift from the owner of one of the markets in the neighbourhood. "I've known that guy all my life," says Trevor. "He sends us oranges and sandwiches whenever he can."

Another one of the answers.

The afternoon is filled with more drills, and only after the drills are there actual games, hard and fast games, real games with sweat and flying snot, the arc of the ball in the air and somebody's elbow in your chest.

Camp ends at 4 p.m. Trevor calls everyone into a circle in the middle of the gym. He tells them what drills he wants them to practise at home. He has them touch hands in the centre of the circle. These kids will sleep hard tonight. You can't get into trouble when you're tired.

"Pride on three," says Trevor.

"One. Two. Three."

"PRIDE!"

After a bit of paperwork, Trevor hops into his car. He has a ten-year-old BMW which has seen better days. The cops stopped him one night because he didn't fit the profile of somebody who owned a BMW. Yeah, right.

Point guards in the States drive Porsches.

Trevor heads downtown. He drives his car the way a point guard takes a ball up court—his eyes are wide open, he sees the traffic develop ahead and positions himself accordingly.

Like a point guard, he also knows how to hustle. Richelieu Knitting has just donated four boxes of T-shirts. Alex, the guy who runs TeeJay printing, is screening the tees for free. Two more answers.

"I need these shirts pretty soon," says Trevor.

"How soon is soon?" says Alex.

"Pronto," says Trevor.

Alex is a basketball rat. He loves the game, he does what he can to help. The shirts will be ready in two days.

Answers to questions.

Last week, somebody called Trevor to ask if he'd like to play for a spot on the national team again—remember, this is Canada's team, the team that will play at the Olympic Games next year. That's as good as it gets for a basketball player in this country.

Trevor passed on the chance. He's got commitments. He'd rather teach kids at the gym. He'd rather stay here, looking for answers to questions.

Watering his roots.

SOMETIMES YOU PUSH, SOMETIMES YOU PULL

At four o'clock in the morning on the docks of the Port of Montreal, you expect rats and shadows and the smell of dirty water. You expect to hear the creak of straining rope, and low moans from the hulls of sleeping ships.

I don't see any rats.

It's a slow morning. Today, the ocean-going *Thorswave* is going to change berths so she can take on a load of scrap. And the *OOCL Bravery*, stacked high with containers, is heading back to Europe. Both ships will need a nudge.

And so the tugboat *Cathy McAllister* wakes up. Across the river, the early sunrise draws itself like a streak of lipstick over the low lights of Longueuil.

"Red sky in the morning, sailor's warning..." says Captain Antoine Tremblay. He drinks his coffee, checks his gear, shows me some charts. "Red sky at night, sailor's delight," I finish for him. "Oh, you know that one," he says. "Maybe it's true. In any case, the sky is only a little red this morning."

We listen to the radio. Captain Tremblay cocks an ear to hear a little better. The port will soon be working at full speed, because the railroad's going back to work—good news for the captain of a tugboat.

Below decks, Jean-Claude LaRivière fires up the engine. He is a small man coaxing a giant, elephant-grey monster to life, and like a mahout he works with utter confidence. Darting here and there, he pushes levers and taps reluctant gauges. The noise of the twelve-hundred horsepower engine blots all the senses.

Our *matelot*, Robert Guevremont, casts off the heavy mooring lines. Tremblay eases the *Cathy* into the oily, olive-green water of the harbour. We smash through the fragile sheets of early morning ice the way a hammer smashes glass.

We're on our way to work.

The tugboat is a masculine device, pure strength built in the service of tenderness. But its strength has nothing to do with speed—we approach the *Thorswave* slowly, inching in beside her as if a bump might startle her and she might run away. Last chance now, no turning back.

Nobody's going anywhere.

There's engine trouble on the *Thorswave.*

We tie up alongside and wait.

Finally we start to move. The big bow thrusters of the saltie push her away from the dock, and then the current catches her and noses her around, and a call comes for us to give the stern a shove.

What's it like, pushing a five-hundred foot container ship? Try easing the bumper of your car up against a four-storey high school. Look carefully both ways to make sure the coast is clear. Then push the school to the other side of the playground.

That's all there is to it.

Go easy on the clutch.

We escort the big ship downstream past others of her kind, past the waiting *Bravery*, past the *Canmar Victory.* Not all the names of ships are names of hope and hubris—we also pass the rusty, battered little *Scarab*—a water strider, or so her owners hope.

By ten to seven, we're turning around again in the current, nudging the *Thorswave* up to the dock. Waiting for her is a mountain of rusty iron, the rotten mainsprings of capitalism ready to be melted down and sold back to us as cars.

When she is finally and securely docked, we chug off to find a quiet spot and wait for our next job. That's when I smell toast. It's time for breakfast.

Below decks, the galley is trim and snug. Suddenly I understand my uncle's kitchen—he was a pilot on the lakes, and he built his wife a galley kitchen just like this one. He must have liked to feel snug.

I'm not sure how my aunt felt.

Here, all the appliances—toaster and microwave, coffeepot and television—are bracketed down so they won't slide around in rough weather. LaRivière pours mugs of coffee, and Captain Tremblay sings to himself. His eggs chuckle in the hot fat of the frying pan.

We take on a new *matelot*, Pierre Niquette. He is lean and intense, the only man to survive when the tug *Patricia B.* went down in the Gulf of St. Lawrence several years ago. Five men died when she sank. I decide it's a good topic not to discuss.

After a meal peppered with jokes and cigarette smoke, and in accordance to Article 12.3 of the collective agreement of the Seamen's Union, the captain of the *Cathy* washes his own dishes. His wedding band shines softly as he dries his plate and cup, the way gold shines on the hand of a man who has been married to his wife and his work for a very long time.

After breakfast, we head down the harbour again, where the *Bravery* awaits. She is a container ship bound for Europe, loaded so high she looks top-heavy. The containers she carries are labelled with conglomerate names—Genstar, Uniflex, Tiphook, Jadropov.

We pick up a line and make fast.

"Sometimes we push, sometimes we pull," says Tremblay. This time we're here to pull. The *Cathy McAllister* digs in, the thick cable stiffens and stretches, then holds. White froth churns up from our stern. It seems as if nothing is happening. And then the *Bravery's* bow begins to swing around toward the open water, and we slip the line free with a splash.

The day's work is done.

On the way back to port, I see the names of men and ships spraypainted on the sides of loading docks. An international calendar, some of the writing is in Cyrillic script and some of it is in Arabic. I read Hernan Paragas, Sonny Guinzon, MV Vishva Shakti.

I ask Niquette if it's a tradition for foreign sailors to make their mark that way. He gives me a serious look. "Yes, it is—and it's forbidden." Then he laughs, the way a man might laugh who's held thoughts of his own about a spray can.

Captain Tremblay fills out his log. It's been a typical day. He says, "You know that TV show, the one about the tugboat? I watch that show. It's very good, quite true to life about what happens in the harbour."

You can take his word for it.

Toot, toot.

The Hungarian Butcher Gets Ready for Easter

The maple block in the cutting room of the butcher shop is old and dark from years of use. It's hollowed as gently as the small of your back. The butcher, Joe Prepszl, holds a sharp knife in his hand.

"Easter is a busy time," he says.

It's ten past seven in the morning. The cutting room is cold and full of pork. There is pork in boxes and buckets, jowls and shoulders and flanks—pink meat, white fat, pale bone.

The room is perfumed with the scent of smoked hams, plump rings of krakowska, dark brown squares of bacon. The Main wakes up to the smell of the Fairmount Meats.

Bela, the butcher's helper—he's a retired mechanic who lends a hand twice a week—pours a couple of buckets of soft white lard into a cauldron. Bela lights a propane heater beneath the giant pot.

Mickey, the butcher's cat, wanders through an open door for a look at the early morning action. Tail high and expectant, Mickey is skinnier than you'd think a butcher's cat would be. "A shop like this needs a cat," says Joe the butcher.

He keeps one eye on his work. The pork is slippery, the knife is sharp. Mickey sniffs at me indifferently, then rubs his head against my jeans and strolls out the door. "He comes and goes," says Joe.

The woman who works in the front of the store arrives at nine. Patsy makes a cup of hot chocolate and sets about her work. She and Joe and Bela are old friends. They've known each other thirty years.

Patsy stocks the shelves in the front of the store with sour cherries and sauerkraut, pickled peppers and paprika, plum jam and chestnut purée.

While the butcher cuts and trims, old men from the neighbourhood peek in for a word or two of Hungarian, a cup of coffee and a smoke, a quick call on the telephone. As the butcher works, his apron reddens.

He wasn't always going to be a butcher. As a young man, he trained to be an artist. But Hungary forty years ago was neither the time nor the place.

Joe's father died in the war. He had seven brothers and sisters at home. An appetite for art is a luxury on an empty stomach.

He reasoned that a butcher always had a bite to eat, so he put down his palette and picked up a cleaver. And then he came to Canada, like so many Hungarians did, in 1956.

The smell of hot lard rises from the cauldron. Bela rubs a tub of square-cut jowls with milk. "It helps to give them colour" he says. Bela pours a bucket of the fatty, milk-splashed meat into the heated lard. An explosion of white steam rises and curls around the room as if it were one of the circles of hell.

Bela stirs the pot with a paddle the size of an oar. Nothing subtle happens in the back room of a butcher shop. He's making what they call fried bacon.

Joe the butcher keeps on cutting. Before the day is through, he'll trim five hundred pounds of meat. It all goes into a mixer, a hundred pink pounds at a time, dusted with handfuls of red paprika, pale green cumin and black pepper.

The colours of the butcher's palette.

Bela grinds the meat, Joe packs it into a hydraulic sausage press and slips a casing over a spout. When he hits the lever, a rope of sausage snakes out. It falls in slick, wet coils on the bench.

Joe pinches and twists the long snake into sausages. Hundreds of dozens of sausages. They'll hang to dry in the cold room, waiting their turn in the smoker.

"You use everything but the tail," I tell the butcher.

He gives me one of those looks.

"We use the tails," he says.

Bela peers into the cauldron at noon, and urges me to eat a piece of rendered pork with a slice of bread. Too rich, I demur. "Most of the fat is melted off," he says. The taste is nutty and complex.

He gives me a slice of warm, pink tongue and watches to see if I like it. Who doesn't like a little warm tongue?

Then Bela takes a fistful of sausage meat the size of a tennis ball and drops it into the lard. When it's crisp and brown, it will be my lunch.

For himself, he takes a slice of bread and passes it through the hot fat, which by now is coloured like strong tea. He gives the bread a moment to drain, then takes a bite. His eyes close from the pleasure of it.

The butcher keeps on working. His lunch, when he finally takes it, is an orange, two bananas and a grapefruit. And a dab or two of sausage meat from time to time, to see if the seasoning's right.

Late in the day, I ask the butcher to show me his hands. He pauses and looks at me hard. He knows what I want to see. The flesh on the back of one finger is bunched up where he sliced it years ago. There is another scar, long and white, running down the back of his hand and across the tops of two fingers.

Sometimes the butcher carves himself.

But not today.

While Bela scrubs the cauldrons and the tubs, Joe the butcher makes up one last special order—the Hungarian Protestant Church needs forty-five pounds of pork jowls, forty-five pounds of liver and sixty pounds of hearts. Food for a celebration.

"Easter is a busy time," says Joe the butcher.

TAXI DRIVER

Augusto Castellon pulls up to the car wash. It's nine o'clock on a Saturday night. He takes the dome light and the aerials from the roof of his cab, a maroon Chevy Caprice, and as the blue rags of the car wash spin and slap, he says, "I always start my night right here."

Can you make a decent living driving a cab, even if it is a clean one? Augusto tells me he pulls in fifty bucks in fares for every hundred kilometres he drives. After expenses, he takes home twenty-five bucks. The margin's small, but some nights are better than others. You do what you can to get ahead. He pulls out into traffic, ready to earn some money.

Saturday's the best night of the week.

Some other Saturday, maybe. Tonight, the weather's warm, and there's no snow on the sidewalks. What's good for you and me is lousy for a cabby.

At ten past ten, an hour after he started work, Augusto finds his first fare of the night, a young man from NDG who wants to go downtown.

The heart of Saturday night begins to beat.

Augusto steps on the gas and heads for the expressway. With a passenger in the back, he drives with purpose, wheeling around the other cars as if they were standing still, and for a brief moment the city sparkles like a fistful of cheap jewels spilled on a black velvet canvas. The kid is a nine dollar fare.

Augusto cruises downtown, scanning the streets for business. He is an easygoing man with a salt and pepper beard and a relaxed smile, but he earns his living the way predators do. He is always moving, always looking for action.

What about the hockey lockout—was it bad for business? "Actually, not so bad," says Augusto. "Maybe sixteen thousand people go to the Forum. Everybody else stays home and watches the

the game on TV. When there is no hockey, I think maybe some of those people go out."

But not many of them are out tonight.

Finally, he spots a couple outside a bar on Ste. Catherine. The man is wearing a windbreaker. He looks ordinary, soft and pleasant.

The woman is something else again. Her face has a frank and direct prettiness. She is professionally made up, and her lips are red and full. She wears expensive earrings, and the bracelets on her wrist make soft noises. She is wearing a fur coat. Her hair is thick and yellow as straw.

The cab pulls into traffic. The woman asks Augusto if she can use his cell phone. She chats briefly, then says, "I'll meet you when I'm finished." It is immediately clear that she is not the man's wife. And if she is his girlfriend, she has not been so for very long, and she will not be so for very long, either.

It is hard not to look at her.

I force myself not to look. Her scent invades the cab. She smells of cigarettes and bar scotch and good perfume, and for a man who simultaneously gave up tobacco and embraced fidelity years ago, the smell is spiced and heady and forbidden.

We drop them near Park LaFontaine and head for the gay village, looking for other fares. By now, it's quarter past eleven, and the streets are very nearly deserted. The only other drivers on the road are empty cabs. Slow night.

We head over to Westmount and back to NDG. For a while, we park at a taxi stand at Walkley and Sherbrooke, killing time beneath an orange and green neon sign, listening to the bark and scratch of the dispatcher.

We talk idly. Augusto says the referendum will be close, but "No" is likely to win. He says he once gave Parizeau a ride. They talked about the taxi business.

What kind of business is it?

Men have stiffed him for fares, a punk or two has tried to hold him up, and women have tried to pay him with something other than money. Augusto is philosophical about it all. Mostly, he doesn't like people who think a cab is a place to eat. He prefers to duck a fare with food. It makes the cab smell bad.

Food isn't the only thing that stinks up the air in a cab. One day he drove past a famous labour leader who tried to flag him down. The labour leader had a cigar in his fist.

Finally, at 1:02 a.m., the dispatcher calls. We pick up a drunk whose face is splashed with gin blossoms. He wants to go three long blocks to a restaurant where he can cash some kind of cheque. He has no money in his pocket. All he has is the cheque. Augusto rolls his eyes. Luckily, they know the drunk at the restaurant.

Three dollar fare.

We prowl the streets of NDG again. Augusto passes the time easily as he drives. He tells me he and his girlfriend take vacations in New Jersey, in a duplex by the ocean. He brings his granddaughters with him. The youngest is barely more than a year. When she wakes for a 5:30 a.m. feeding, he gives her a bottle and takes her in his arms and walks with her on the beach.

Suddenly, two girls in their early twenties climb in for a short ride up the Main. Immediately after that, a young couple flags us down. He's huge and she's tiny. They get out at separate addresses in the east end.

Business picks up as the bars begin to close. A light snow falls as we drop a couple of college kids on a quiet street near the Oratory. They are the best fare of the night.

Back on the Main, the cops have set up a roadblock outside the bar Eugene Patin. The cops are checking cars for alcohol. Augusto sails on through. "Cabs don't have to stop for this," he says.

We take a fare north past Little Italy and then we luck on another fare right after that, a fat man near the Sauvé métro. And then things slack off again. Rush hour's over. We head back to headquarters. It's 4:30 in the morning.

In the dim quiet of the office, the dispatcher shows me a pile of paper slips with scribbled annotations. Bus ticket. Wallet. Purse. Laundry bag. These are some of the things customers have forgotten in the back seats of Diamond cabs today.

The list contains none of the items of taxi legend—once a woman forgot two suitcases full of antique handguns in a cab; the guns were reckoned to be worth three hundred thousand dollars.

Once someone left behind a set of false teeth. Somebody else forgot his crutches. One person left a wheelchair in the trunk. These remarkable lapses of memory have become stock stories, recounted with humour and disbelief.

This year, there was an addition to the roster—just before Christmas, a woman left two bags of presents in the trunk of a Diamond cab. The dispatcher rolls his eyes.

After a bottle of tomato juice and a few more stories, Augusto's evening ends. It's been a long night. He's driven 162 kilometres. He's had eight fares.

He takes home $54.30.

NIGHT SHIFT ON THE MAIN

Soft rain is falling on fresh snow. On the corner of the street, a young woman in a yellow slicker wades through a black puddle. Down the block, a pack of university kids chuck snowballs back and forth in the dark.

All the lights are on in all the restos on the street, and all the waiters are waiting at their stations, nervous as greyhounds before a race. The night shift is about to begin.

In the upstairs kitchen on the second floor of a smoked meat palace called The Main, a Salvadoran named Merino splashes water in a double sink. He is a happy man. During the day, he works as a presser at a coat factory. At night he works here, washing pots.

Merino's day is seventeen hours long. He is twenty-two years old. Why is he smiling? His wife has just given birth to their second child.

Peter Varvaro isn't as young as Merino, but he works nearly as many hours. He owns The Main. He'll be cutting steaks until midnight, and he'll be back at work at ten tomorrow morning. He looks a little tired now.

What's the strangest thing that's ever happened on the night shift? Peter considers the question as he pushes a rib steak past the blade of the band saw. He's seen his share of louts and goofs, so many that they have become one lout, one goof. There have been robberies, two of them.

Then he remembers: A woman came into the restaurant one evening in the old days, years ago. She ordered a big meal, finished it, wiped her lips and then she walked out into the middle of the street and took off all her clothes.

The cops took her away.

At nine, Barbara joins the two men in the upstairs kitchen. Barbara is the chef. She has a glass of coffee in one hand, a forbidden cigarette in the other. Her gaze is steady and unblinking.

Barbara is slim, in her thirties. She's dressed in a white sweater, a short apron and blue slacks. She learned to cook in Poland.

She takes six briskets out of the cooler and rubs them with salt and pepper. She layers the meat in roasting pans, and bathes them with oil. She chops onions, celery and carrots on top of the briskets. Into the oven they go.

She wipes the stainless steel counter, then sets a pot of water on the stove. She takes a bucket of liver and two dozen eggs from the cooler. She starts to fry a pot of onions. She boils the eggs. The liver—dark, thick and slippery—slides into the heat of a second oven.

Now she fills another pot with water. You could bathe in this pot, it is so big. With Merino's help, she sets it on the stove. She tosses in dozens of beef ribs, adds a splash of salt, a handful of garlic, and turns on the gas burner.

She gives the onions a stir. The air smells begins to smell salty-sweet. Does she cook like this at home? "Yes, my husband is a very lucky man."

Last night, Barbara made a million latkes, matzoh balls and kishkas. She boiled more tongues than spoke at the tower of Babel. She made enough rice pudding and blintzes to satisfy the hunger of a thousand of those tongues.

Tonight she'll make a million varenekes, pronounced veronicas. You know them as perogies. No matter. Barbara takes a sip of coffee, shells her hardboiled eggs, and turns the liver in the oven. She doesn't stop.

Now she cores, quarters and slices seven heads of cabbage, some onions and some carrots. She mixes two gallons of dressing and voila!—coleslaw, glistening like cut hay in the rain. Peter and Merino go home. Barbara is just getting started.

Downstairs in one of the booths, a big woman talks to herself as she eats a pair of smoked meat sandwiches. The Main is practically empty. She should talk to the grill man. He's bored stiff. It's only midnight. It's still early.

Barbara wipes her forehead with the back of her hand. She sighs in one of the five languages she speaks, and assembles what she needs for the chopped liver. She passes the hardboiled eggs through the grinder. They fall into a basin, yellow and pale as daisies in a field.

Now the booths downstairs are suddenly full, and they will stay full until 4:00 a.m. The grillman is slathering mustard, he's slicing steamy sandwiches for dozens of sleepless old men, for kids with illegal smiles, for punks and drunks and yuppies. They are a democracy of empty stomachs in a parliament of smoked meat. Some honourable members are starved.

I spy a well-dressed couple. The man has good hair and manners, the woman is shy. She spears a french fry with a silver fork. Her lips are swollen, scarlet. The tip of the fry is painted red with ketchup. She takes a dainty bite. The eros of that gesture.

Back upstairs, Barbara is rolling a sheet of dough and cutting circles for the varenekes. She fills one circle with a mixture of potatoes, onions and cheese. She folds it over and pinches it stylishly shut. She will do this fifteen dozen times.

It's early morning now. The chopped liver has been packed in tubs, the ribs and roasts are chilled, the buckets of cole slaw and the trays of varenekes put away.

A solitary couple slides into a booth downstairs. He has the bright eyes of a sled dog. She is pale, nearly albino, and she holds a blood-red rose in her hand. The effect is vaguely disturbing, as if the rose had leached the complexion from her cheeks. They order breakfast.

Barbara wipes her last counter. She comes downstairs and says goodnight to the waiters. She picks up a loaf of bread from the bakery down the street and heads for home. The man with the sled-dog eyes lights up another smoke. The white-blonde woman asks for more coffee.

The night shift comes to an end.

FIT TO BE TIED

The room is knotted with single guys and Brad-and-Janet couples. They are making their way through the darkness. They are making their way past the others.

The others wear leather chokers and leather chaps, latex vests and bras, and motorcycle hats. These others cut through the dark with an air of cool and benign menace. And in their midst, I wander aimlessly. I am trying not to betray intent.

I am at Flesh. It is billed as an exotic, erotic voyeur's ball.

I'm just looking.

I watch a woman wearing a leather harness and not much else climb atop a podium. A man begins to hit her gently with a horsetail whip. This is the warm-up act. She adopts a set of voguish postures while he works.

He isn't actually whipping. He flicks and he caresses. He, too, betrays no intent. He looks as if he'd rather be doing something else. Her head remains bent throughout the performance. The Brads and Janets seem bored.

But you can't tell much by looking.

On my way to get a beer, I bump into an elderly man in a studded choker, studded gloves and not much else. He himself is studded. Seven times in each ear. He is barechested and studded there, too.

His arms are slight and tanned. He's begun to soften like a piece of fruit that's been left too long on the shelf. He looks as menacing as an apple doll.

I glance at several booths around the perimeter of the room. One displays chain mail bikinis and metal devices whose uses I cannot guess at. Another dispenses black-and-white brochures describing various kinds of physical restraints.

I see a photo of a form-fitting latex body bag. From the photo, I can tell there is a person in the bag. The bag is criss-crossed with ropes. Whoever's in the bag is tied down in the rubber darkness as thoroughly as Gulliver.

I try to imagine myself wanting to be enveloped in a latex bag. I try to imagine wanting to truss up some other person in a bag. It must be dark and sweaty in there. Is helplessness the attraction?

I'd like to ask somebody, but I'm not sure how to phrase the question. I'm also just the tiniest bit apprehensive. There is a good possibility any question I have in this room will be misunderstood.

I'm trying to understand.

The phrase "whatever turns you on" won't swell large enough to cover what I see next—a photo of another bag, this time a heavy-duty mail sack hanging suspended from a leather belt. From the lumpiness, it appears there is someone crouched inside.

My dad delivered mail for twenty-three years. During that time, he never spoke about the urge to clamber inside his sack and hang there in the dark, suspended from a hook like so many undelivered letters.

But you never know.

The room is slow to fill up. Tardiness seems to be in keeping with the nature of the event. The air is thick with the musky tension between wanting and waiting.

I'm surprised by the number of people in costume. I'm not sure why I'm surprised. Then my eye is caught by a cheerful young woman who fairly bulges out of a skimpy, black vinyl top.

My eye is also caught by a young man in a white shirt and shoes and socks, and not much else. He may be wearing some sort of diaper. I can't tell. His shirt tails are too long. He's white-guy pale. The flashing lights make him look paler. I don't get it.

You can't tell much by looking.

The first act of the night is a drag singer in a sequinned emerald-green dress. She looks good, but she hasn't got enough hips. Her hair is shoulder length, combed off the face, flipped at the ends.

She sings a bitter little ballad, one of those love-gone-wrong songs. Once again, I think of my old man. He was a dance-band musician when he wasn't delivering mail. He played trombone and he sang those set-'em-up Joe songs at the close of each set. He had a smokey, whisky voice.

The diva in the green dress pokes sly fun at the music, but she can't sing half as well as my old man. Off-key and off-colour, she can't sing well enough to make it work.

Sorry, Pop.

She approaches the edge of the stage and grabs a guy's beer. She takes a long, deep swig and gives the bottle back. The guy wants to be cool. He also doesn't want to drink any more from that particular bottle.

The second act is a man with a bag of whips, in the company of a healthy, happy-looking young woman. She wears leather chaps, a vest and a cowboy hat. She holds a balloon in each hand.

He flicks a whip at the balloons. One of them breaks, and scatters a shower of sparkle dust. Nice effect, but the other one won't break, not even after several direct hits. The audience is giggling. He's not pleased. It is embarrassing.

Finally, he takes the balloon from her and puts it on the floor and breaks it with his heel. The audience cheers.

The third act is more serious and, if you will, more successful.

A woman in a torso bag is led out on a chain. What is this thing with bags? The chain is attached like a leash at her neck. The bag is a straightjacket with a hood. She's in the dark.

The man who holds the chain wears a body harness. He is followed by a man wearing leather shorts, rubber hip waders and a fireman's hat, and another man in a harness and gloves. The men are carrying tool kits.

They release the woman from the torso bag. Although she wears a variety of chains and buckles, she is fundamentally unclothed. The men attach her to a trapeze and hoist her off the floor. She is standing on the bar. Her arms and legs are spread.

The man who led her out begins to spank her rhythmically with a stiff, black belt. He isn't fooling. The belt is thick and hard. From where I stand, more than fifty feet away, I can see the red welts raised on her rump.

When he finishes, he takes an electric clipper and shaves her armpits and her scalp. He lights three candles and drips hot wax on her. Finally, he stubs out the candles on her skin. He stubs the candles quickly, with a short stabbing motion. She doesn't flinch. I do. At a distance, I can see the burn marks.

Her face remains impassive, but her eyes are large and liquid. They contain a mixture of humiliation and utter trust.

It's hard to tell by looking, but I think I understand what's going on from an intellectual point of view. There is a subtle interplay between what he does and what she lets him do. I think it is possible for there to be pain and power and pleasure on both sides of the equation. And then I think, so what?

I don't wait for the final acts.

I walk through the cool air to the métro. Riding home, I find myself sitting across from a kid in a dirty, zippered motorcycle jacket. The sight of the innocent leather makes me smile. But it is a nervous smile.

Because you can't tell much by looking.

BULLET WOUNDS AND BANDAIDS

The telephone rings, and someone shouts and runs toward an operating room. An elderly Jamaican woman sits up in her bed. She looks around, as if she's not sure where she is. This is Emergency. This is the Royal Vic.

"Chest wound coming in!"

Dr. Robert Foxford, who is young and slim and handsome enough to be a TV doctor, issues a series of orders clearly and simply and quickly. Nurses and interns snap to attention. This is not TV.

Someone shouts, "Here he is!"

Two wide doors swing open, and a large young man is wheeled in on a stretcher. He is overweight, wide-eyed, sweating. He's sitting up and breathing hard. Half his shirt is off. He's looking at the doctors and the nurses who are swarming over him.

He's trying to read their faces, to see if he's going to die. Not if they can help it. They shift him onto an operating table, jab him with needles, hook him to a monitor. He says, "J'ai mal. J'ai mal."

I can see a round red spot on his ribs. The bullet wound. It looks as if someone has stubbed out a cigarette six inches under his armpit. It looks harmless enough, except it dribbles blood.

"Uff," the man grunts, "J'ai mal."

He wants to show us he's a tough guy who can take it, but he seems surprised that he has to. This is not TV. This hurts too much.

As suddenly as he was surrounded, everyone scuttles away. The X-ray machine shoots a picture, and everyone scuttles back in. The man and all the rest of us look at the ghostly picture of the bullet. It has travelled across his body. It rests in his left side.

Now a doctor quickly drives a needle into the wound, and cuts a slit in the skin with a knife. He pushes a tube through the slit, pushes it high up into the man's chest. The doctor leans in hard. The tube is as thick as a finger. Blood from the wound drains out. The man is awake through it all. "J'ai mal," he says, "j'ai mal." And then he's wheeled off to another operating room so the surgeons can get the bullet out.

Emergency calms down.

There are stomachs to pump here, cuts to stitch, there are bruises to poke and prod. The Jamaican woman stands up.

In the bed next to her is a tentative, grey-haired man. He has problems with his vision, his balance. He is embarrassed to be here. Foxford makes him stand, makes him walk around the bed. The man walks as if he's on a tightrope. Foxford orders a CAT scan. The man may have had a stroke. He is my father's age. This is not TV.

Down the hall in another bed, a man whose foot is grossly swollen. He says it hurts like hell. I believe it does. It looks like it's about to burst. Foxford asks, "What happened?" The man says he was at the muffler shop. The hoist that raised his car was lowered on his toe.

After the chest wound, this is comic relief.

The telephone rings again. Someone wants to know if the man who was shot is okay. Foxford snaps, "Don't say anything. The guy on the phone could be the shooter. You never know."

You never know in Emerge.

A woman from Housekeeping pulls a mask across her mouth and mops the isolation room. She says to no one in particular, "I haven't had a break. My head is getting a headache." Nobody offers her aspirin. A headache's not an emergency.

Foxford sends the crushed toe home. He looks at an old woman who's been brought in reeking of urine. She smiles. Her front teeth are missing. She is delusional. Foxford smells psychosis, and orders every test in the book.

Suddenly the hospital is surrounded by cop cars. Word is, the gang with the gun is coming to finish the job. Foxford takes a deep breath and scribbles some notes. The air smells of shit and disinfectant, and now it smells of fear. This is not TV.

The Jamaican woman falls down.

Foxford says, "Damn, she was supposed to be stable." The cops will take care of the gang. He will take care of her.

At midnight, he hands the patients over to Dr. Mitch Shulman.

Shulman is a lithe and bearded dynamo. He spins back and forth, non-stop, from acute care to minor care and back again. In the centre of his own whirlwind, he is calm. He has to be. It doesn't stop. There's no time out for commercial breaks.

A man who hasn't had a drink in twenty days begins to vomit blood. A man with no symptoms except chronic pain needs someone to tell him not to worry. Shulman treats them equally, carefully. It's a long night. He's working on his own. Finally there is a lull.

It's temporary.

The bars have closed down. The action picks up. A bouncer from a nightclub waits quietly in a wheelchair with a bloody bandage around his forehead. Someone jabbed a broken glass in his face. Shulman takes a look. He calls for a plastic surgeon.

A young man, a suicide attempt, lies shaking on a stretcher. His legs and arms jiggle under their restraints. His eyes are closed. His father paces the hall by himself, and smiles.

Suddenly the waiting room fills up with a crowd of muscular, angry young men. They move with menacing gravity. They are well-dressed and polite, through gritted teeth. They are colleagues of the man whose face was jabbed. They crowd the narrow corridor. They're in the way. They want to see their friend. Nothing's going to stop them.

Nothing except Shulman. He looks up at them and says, "Not all at once." He only has to say it once. They give him due respect.

Finally the sun comes up.

I ask a passing surgeon about the man who was shot. He says, "Two holes in the liver, two in the large intestine, one hole in the stomach." Is he going to make it? "We'll know in a couple of days."

A man from housekeeping sweeps the floors. The pillow of the bouncer is stained red, in the shape of a map of France. The Jamaican woman has gone home with her daughter. The father of the overdose sits quietly and stares at cartoons on the TV in the waiting room. He smiles, but he looks so very sad.

Shulman takes a deep breath.

BERSON'S

Mendy Berson answers the phone. It is the first call of the morning. His voice is calm and quiet. Nobody calls him without a serious reason. He is the owner of Berson's Monuments.

He listens carefully, and nods his head and makes a note on a pad. The caller asks a simple question, to which Mendy replies, "The stonecutters know Hebrew. If they didn't, I'd be in trouble."

There is no trouble here today.

Nor is there with the dead, any day—they are past caring. It's up to the living to make monuments in their memory. It is a tedious and sobering process.

Today, there are half a dozen stones laying flat on old sawhorses, waiting for their inscriptions. The wooden floor groans under their weight. I look closely at one of the stones. The polished surface is shiny as a mirror, and I see the reflection of something familiar.

My face on a headstone.

Yikes.

Hanging here and there on the walls of the shop are patterns for Stars of David, Hebrew alphabets in various sizes, patterns for roses, lilies, candles. Elsewhere there are cupboards crammed with record books holding seventy years' worth of names and dates and inscriptions. Berson's is nothing if not a classroom for the study of life and death, and love and grief, among the Jews of Montreal.

I ask Mendy if he's had any unusual requests for inscriptions or for headstone decoration. He remembers one woman who wanted a ball of yarn with knitting needles on her stone, and a man who wanted a bass leaping out of the water, but most stones are plain and most epitaphs are slight—a few words, two dates.

It's fitting, in a way, that the stones are so heavy—each one weighs a thousand pounds—because the epitaph it carries will last longer than the life it describes.

Here are some of the epitaphs the stonecutters are writing today:
A Survivor of the Holocaust. Husband, Father and Grandfather.
Loved and Remembered Forever. A Man of Compassion, Honour
and Charity. Always in Our Hearts.

A serious young woman named Olga Frangoulis runs the letter
press. She bends over her work, laying out an unusually long
inscription which, for an epitaph, reads like a chapter of a novel:
"And Joseph sustained his father and his brothers and all his father's
household with bread."

Olga, do you ever make a mistake? "Not many." Does a mistake
ever get onto a stone? "Sometimes." What happens then? "We do a
new one." She is a woman of few words. She speaks epitaph.

One of the stonecutters lays a pattern on a headstone for an old
woman who knew years of grief. The design is taken from a rubbing
made at her husband's grave. Her husband died 30 years ago. The
headstones have to match. "Nobody dies together," says Mendy.

Not everyone dies so far apart.

Mendy's grandfather Al started Berson's Monuments in 1922.
He was tired of hauling sacks of coal up flights of stairs. Al's son
Hyman took over full-time in 1946. Mendy took over from him in
1973. It's a family business, but fathers and sons rarely see eye to eye.
Mendy and Hyman had two differences of opinion:

Hyman had built a dust collector to gather up the clouds of
powdered stone that billowed from the sandblaster. He thought it
worked fine but it was old and out of date, and there was dust
blowing all over the Main. Mendy had seen the city inspectors
hovering. He knew the dust collector wasn't working fine.

And then there was the business of the letter-press. In Hyman's
day, they'd cut epitaph stencils by hand. Mendy wanted to buy a
mechanical letter-press. The two men argued themselves into an
uneasy standoff. Mendy asked his mother for advice. "Wait," she
said. He waited.

When Hyman went on vacation one November, Mendy put in
the new dust collector. Then he bought the letter press.

Mendy's father came back from Florida in May and took a taxi
to the shop. Work stopped when he arrived. Everyone wanted to see
the fireworks when the old man walked in the door.

Hyman Berson looked at the dust collector. Then he looked at
the letter press. And then he looked at Mendy. One of the helpers

showed the old man how the letter press worked. It was an improvement.

The two Bersons went back to the office together. Mendy sat at the desk. Nobody said a word. Then Mendy's father spoke. "You made changes without my consent." Mendy said nothing. Hyman looked out the window.

Then the old man saw his taxi driver stepping out of Schwartz's. The cabbie paused and wiped the grease from a smoked meat sandwich off his lips. Hyman Berson walked out the door and hailed the driver and went back home in the cab he'd come in. The office telephone rang a little later. It was Mendy's mother. "Your father just retired," she said.

If you know what to look for in the shop, you can see some of the sociology of life and death in Montreal. You can also see the remains of the struggle between three generations of Berson men. It is a struggle which dates from the days when the stones were cut with wire saws, and letters were chiselled by hand.

Times change. These days, stones are ordered pre-cut. And while that old dust collector still works, the letter press has been rendered out-of-date by the computer. Alas, Mendy has no sons to force change on him. Will his daughter take over the business? He shrugs his shoulders. You never know.

She has a degree in Jewish studies.

STANLEY LEWIS

To get to work, the sculptor Stanley Lewis has to climb a flight of wooden stairs set in the middle of a field of granite tombstones. The tombstones lie squarely in the yard of Berson's Monuments, above which Stanley rents a corner loft.

The stairs are wooden. They wobble. The tombstones are greyish, solid, and blank. They remind the sculptor of his own mortality.

Ars longa, Lewis brevis.

There is a naked woman in the studio. Mendy Berson says he's not surprised at the goings-on upstairs. "Stanley Lewis is quite a lady's man. I could tell you stories to make your hair stand on end." Berson doffs his cap. The top of his head is smooth.

The woman in question is made of pink marble. There is a cleft running up the length of her, an extension of the cleft between her legs. As a result, this cold stone woman is as shocking and frankly erotic as a piece of fruit, a seashell or a woman made of flesh.

Stanley Lewis carves this cleft as if his life depended on it; hers does. He uses a fine chisel, straightening the line here and there, following it until it splits the space between her marble breasts, dividing her in two as surely as the Main splits Montreal.

Each tap of the hammer produces a puff, a breath of marble dust. The sculptor uses a tempered chisel and a soft iron hammer. You can tell how the work is going by the rhythm of the blows.

You can hear the pinging of the stone, as if it were a bell. If there was no ping, if he heard a click, he would know the stone was flawed. There are no flaws in this stone. It is marble, rosa aurora, from Portugal. It is flesh-coloured. In the light of day, it has the warmth of skin.

After a series of short, sharp hammer blows, Lewis runs one long chisel-stroke up the length of the cleft to unify the line. The hammer he uses is Italian. The chisel is one he made himself. Now he picks up a rasp and smoothes the skin of a thigh. The rasp is Chinese.

He stands as he works, his legs spread wide and bent at the knee. He thrusts his pelvis forward. He is constantly touching the work, chipping, smoothing, rasping, feeling the form of the stone as if his hands could bring it to life.

As he taps again with hammer and chisel, the torso on the wooden bench rocks back and forth. The picture you see is one of a small square man dancing a sexual waltz with a large naked stone in a small cold room.

On every surface of the studio there is litter—pieces of chalk, bits of pencils and crayon, masks and filters, tins of turpentine, jugs of soap and plastic bottles of motor oil. There are piles of chisels and hammers and rasps, there are brushes and rags. There is dust on everything.

And everywhere you look there are completed sculptures. Everything Lewis has done for the past ten years is here. There are white marble heads, there are stone assemblages, and there are fossil-like forms made from hard black stone.

This black stone is not from Carrara, nor the far north. He found it on top of a heap of excavation near the Royal Vic. One night he drove by the hospital and saw piles of it glistening in the rain. Montreal limestone. He came back with a truck. The stone is hard, and it polishes beautifully.

As the sculptor works, I look at his hands. They are blunt, and there is a huge squat muscle at the base of each thumb. Look at the muscle below your own thumb. If you were to double in size, it still would not be as large as Stanley's.

This muscle is the hallmark of a sculptor who, for control, holds hammer and chisel with a "thumbs-up" grip.

As the sculptor shapes the stone, so the stone shapes the sculptor. He turns his hands over, shows me his palms. There are ragged scars running from the base of each palm to each wrist, the result of surgery to relieve carpal tunnel syndrome.

They are not elegant scars. It looks as the doctor used a pocketknife to give the sculptor one more inch of lifeline. Which, in a sense, is what happened. A sculptor who can't use his hands is not a sculptor.

Now Stanley Lewis wets one of the pink breasts with a rag. Dust constantly obscures his work; a quick wash lets him see the stone as it will look when it is polished. The tip of the breast drips chalky water.

It might as well be milk. Stanley says he had a recent visit from a woman with a child. The child reached instantly for the marble breasts. Lewis felt, at that moment, as if he had succeeded.

He's been working on this stone for months. He's had it since June of '94. It weighed five hundred pounds. He stared at it every day. And then, on August 16th of this year, he started work. He's been working on it daily ever since.

There are pictures and drawings on every wall of the studio. I see a scrap of paper with a quotation from Goethe: "Every day look at a beautiful picture, read a beautiful poem, listen to beautiful music, and, if possible, say some reasonable thing."

Now Stanley Lewis runs his palm over the torso's flank, where the stone is mottled with grey. The darker the stone, the harder the marble—when he runs a chisel up the thigh, he must vary the strength of each blow to ensure an even cut.

"Look," he says. "See this white dot on the stone?" I'm not sure that I do. I suppose there is a sort of white blemish the size of a pinprick in the marble. He says, "This white dot means a crystal in the stone is bruised. I've got to take it out, or else you'll see it when it's polished." He says this process is called civilising the stone.

Sounds beautiful, sounds reasonable to me.

WHAT YOU SEE IS WHAT YOU GET

A little middle-aged guy was reading a magazine in a newsstand. He was one of a million, the kind of guy who wouldn't stick out in a crowd unless he stuck a naked chicken on his head and made it cluck.

His head was bowed, his attitude reverential. He had skinny arms, he wore a crumpled shirt, his mousy hair lay slicked on top of his bald spot. On the face of it, he wasn't worth a second look. But I am a nosy guy.

I wanted to see what he was reading.

He held the magazine at arm's length. The poor man, I suppose his eyes are going—that's what I thought as I walked by. I sympathized with him. My eyes are going, too.

But they're still pretty good.

They're good enough to see that he was staring at a colour photo of a young guy with big muscles and no clothes on, who was holding his swollen self in his hands. It was something to see. I did a double take. Either the man in the photo had very small hands or a very big self.

I do not normally expect, in the course of my day, to see a photo like this staring back at me. The sight of it was absurd, like the thought of the naked chicken on the man's head.

I very nearly giggled.

It was all too incongruous. This skinny little man who ached to hold the muscles of the man in the magazine, in the middle of a newsstand on a sunny afternoon, was like the mouse who wanted the elephant.

And then I felt embarrassed at what I saw, and then I felt stupid because I felt embarrassed. I looked away because what should have been private had suddenly become public, and it was none of my business. After all, everybody likes to look, and he was looking at what he liked. No harm done. Whatever turns you on.

But it was my business, in a way, because I'd seen it and because there are times when an accidental faceful of pornography doesn't always produce a suppressed giggle. Sometimes it produces suppressed rage.

The last time she and I were in a newsstand buying papers, she happened to look over someone's shoulder, too, and saw a photo of a woman lying on her back, naked as a jaybird, knees up, in full colour.

There was a look of agony or ecstasy on the face of the woman in the magazine. She lay in the posture of birth, except she wasn't pregnant, and the man who was looking at the photo didn't have paternity in mind.

We stormed out of the newsstand, which is to say she stormed and I followed. I understand why she was upset. We're all voyeurs, but this is not a culture of dominant women looking at submissive men. It's the other way around.

Opportunities to look are everywhere, and she and a lot of other women and some men don't much like it. But there is no escape. This is a culture of male horniness.

And maybe we are too publicly, too visually, permissive. It could have been your son or daughter looking at what we saw in that newsstand. It could have been your son or daughter in those magazines.

Much will have more; Emerson said that. Men can't help staring anywhere, at any time, it's a knee-jerk reaction; I said that. Yeah, and staring at pictures is for jerks; she said that.

There are jerks all over.

On a mid-day stroll through the lingerie section of any major Canadian department store, you can sometimes see the lonely single men, often but not always elderly, prowling the causal aisles for a peek at the mannequin décolletage, the lanky plaster thighs in garter belts, the pale toes in silk stockings.

These must be men who can't afford a magazine.

I know they are there. I've seen them drooling over the pictures on the boxes that the bras come in. What was I doing in the lingerie section of a major Canadian department store?

Just looking.

These days, when we are in newsstands, I find myself shielding her from the section where the girlie books are kept. It is an indirect shielding. I simply try to keep myself between her and them.

So I can I keep the peeks to myself, I suppose.

And these days when we go shopping together, I bring something to read in case she gets the urge to buy some *sous-vêtements*. That way I can sit quietly somewhere and keep my head down.

I'm not proud of the fact that I steal automatic glances at scantily-clad mannequins. Mannequins are somehow lower down the scale than pictures in magazines. I still gawk. So does every other man you know. Stupid, eh?

As we walked home from the newsstand, I imagined what it would be like if I were surrounded in my daily life by pictures of pouty men panting on their knees or sucking their fingers. I thought it would be ridiculous. The thought of it made me suppress another giggle.

"What are you giggling at?" she said.

"Nothing," I replied.

MARTHE TURGEON

The actress Marthe Turgeon smiles, and in her smile it is possible to see both the overlay of beauty, and the underpinning of intelligence, in her face.

I've asked her age.

It is certainly not the most difficult question she's had to answer. Three men have proposed to her. She said yes to one, and then quickly changed her mind. Marriage is a question, and a dare, with a greater degree of risk.

Now she appraises me, as if to consider whether I, like the unlucky three, have the nerve to hear what she has to say. "I'm fifty," she says. Her voice is one part smoke and one part lion's purr, daring me to ask her more.

She is the youngest child of a handsome man who liked to sing when he had a drink. She implies that he sang more often than she would have liked. She knew she would act when she was eight, as soon as she saw her first movie. She decided that, since she had no control over life as it swirled around her, she'd control her life on stage.

Twenty-five years ago, fresh from acting school in Quebec, Marthe came to Montreal as if it were a foreign country. She arrived here as a single mother. She's made a living as an actor ever since.

She is about to appear on stage in an English-language play. Her role is that of a Quebecker who retreats to Westmount, as if that were a foreign country.

To work on your art, work on your life.

Marthe does an hour of physical exercise before today's rehearsal. It is a way to release the tension, to undo the knots, to allow her to approach the stage with a clear mind and a ready body. She stretches, cycles, and sweats in the steamroom of a downtown hotel.

I wait for her on the roof-top terrace, and read a book on acting technique. A wave of bees passes over me, hovering, sniffing, ready to probe, ready to sting. I feel them nudge my arm, my wrist, my hand.

The job of an actor is to present, it is not to represent. I present myself as something which is neither threat nor promise to a bee.

The bees buzz off.

Good acting.

Marthe drives across town to rehearsal. She is refreshed, relaxed, dressed in black from head to toe. Her mind as clear as pure air. But driving is not acting; she does not follow the rules of the road as much as she blurts forward when there is an opportunity.

Now she blurts into a corner gas station. The little island is crowded, it is late in the afternoon. She begins to back up, in order to approach the pump at a proper angle.

Thunk.

Marthe sighs.

Where did that car come from? The other driver, an older man, is annoyed. He did not expect to have an accident at a gas station, and he expects the worst sort of damage—which is to say, less than the deductible.

He gets out of his car slowly, and Marthe get out of hers. Together they look at the front of his car. There is a mark on the rim of the front wheel, nothing more. Is it possible no damage was done?

He and Marthe take a closer look, and she is at once the man's insurance agent and mechanic, attending to his car, handling his case briskly. "This is no problem here, don't you agree?" she says.

He is about to melt, and is considering a gallant reply, when two guys in tight silk shirts pass by on the sidewalk. They notice the tableau. They rush right over, fairly popping their buttons, certain they've been presented with a damsel in distress.

One of them attends to Marthe, preparing to offer his arm. The other examines the scratch on the rim of the wheel. "There is no problem here," they say, looking at her and defying the old man to disagree.

The old man is not amused. It is definitely not for them to say there is no problem. Besides, if this woman is in any distress, he will provide her with comfort himself; after all, it's his car that was hit.

"I've got no problem with you," he says to Marthe as he stands up, wiping his hands. "But I have a problem with these two telling me there's no problem."

It is suddenly complicated.

The two guys in tight shirts roll their shoulders. They look at each other, they open their mouths and close their fists and swell their chests. Marthe says once again that there is no problem with either of the cars, but now the two guys in silk shirts are bouncing up and down on the balls of their feet.

The tension breaks when another car drives up. The driver honks his horn. He would like to get some gas, if you don't mind. The man who owns the car with the dinged wheel has to move to let him in.

Now the two guys in the tight shirts can hear the air leaking out of their balloon. There is no percentage in hassling the old man. They look at Marthe, but she has forgotten them and is busy paying for her gas. They walk away, bandy-legged. One of the guys puts a hand on his crotch, and walks like an ape down the street.

Bad acting.

Marthe continues on her way without incident.

Rehearsal is up three flights of stairs. The floor of the hall is dirty black, taped to show the outline of a stage. Marthe paces the set, she marks her place. She is an athlete of the spirit preparing for the start of a race. There is a sense of energy gathering.

The director sits off-stage, amid bottles of water and cans of pop, full ashtrays, notebooks, a stopwatch, a pack of smokes, a lighter and a métronome. The script requires Marthe's character to remember some forgotten song her father used to sing.

Now, standing on the apron of the stage, Marthe speaks her lines as if there were a hint of her father's face in hers, and in her voice an air of his wild song.

For a moment she is neither an actress of fifty nor a girl of eight, but a woman caught flickering somewhere in between. She finishes her lines, abruptly lights a cigarette and turns away.

I am aware that I have not breathed since she began to speak.

MAKING A LIVING

Two neighbourhood kids in baseball caps come into the dépanneur. The short kid carries a pair of skates and a gym bag on his shoulder. The tall kid flips two quarters on the counter. He's hip, he watches them spin. He says, "Two cancers, please."

So much for the health warnings.

The man who owns the dépanneur is Vietnamese. He is slight and small but he looks strong. His eyes are soft and so is his smile. He takes two cancers from an open pack. The kids light up, and head off into the rain.

Welcome to the world. Welcome to Thach's dépanneur.

That's Thach, pronounced talk.

Isn't it illegal, selling cancers one stick at a time? "Yes, but we all do it. If I don't do it, my customers give me hell." When you measure your profit in nickels and dimes, you don't want your customers giving you hell.

Thach will sell you a dog leash if you want, and a videotape and a slinky toy and a tin of Italian-style poutine. He'll sell you a plastic banana filled with banana-flavoured powder—this is a kind of candy. If you want, you can buy a bag of chips supposed to taste like a pizza, a BLT or a burger. I've no idea why you'd want to.

An old man in a raincoat comes into the store. He buys a bag of peanuts in the shell. "Not for me," he laughs. "Going to feed the squirrels in the park."

There's a copy of the latest *Police Plus* on the magazine stand. In it is the story of a woman forced to quit school on account of her breasts. It seems they were too big. The photo on the cover would appear to support her claim. She doesn't look as if she's sorry she had to quit.

When Thach and I first met, he was sitting by his cash register doing what looked like homework. I thought, "Here's an immigrant's story." I asked him if he was taking night courses.

He said he was preparing math homework, not for himself but for his sons. He teaches the boys a year ahead at home, so they'll do well at school. A better story than I thought. His boys are getting good grades. They won't drop out of school.

Thach scratches out a living selling *Police Plus* and the usual staples—a litre of homo, a can of beer, a pack of cigarettes, the daily papers. He makes a dime on a litre of milk, thirty cents on a pack of smokes.

He'll even sell you a condom, although he says he doesn't sell too many. "Maybe five or ten a year," he smiles. This doesn't say much for the virility or the common sense of the men and women of Plateau Mont-Royal.

Thach smiles a lot. His smile is why we go there, instead of half a dozen other places in the neighbourhood. When Thach smiles, we feel good.

Enter a ten year old with the air of a man of affairs. He has money in his fist. He's here on business. He buys a quart of two per cent and "a pack of Players for my Dad." With the change he buys a Bazooka gum and stuffs it in his mouth.

He is about to leave when something catches his eye. He sees the face of a little girl on a Cystic Fibrosis donations box. She looks at him. He melts. He gives her a couple of coppers.

Two minutes later he's back and chewing hard. "Do you have any eggs?" He buys a dozen, and gets another Bazooka with the change. He stuffs it in his mouth, on top of the first. The sweet smell of gum fills the air.

Hanging from the ceiling of the dépanneur, the men in the flying canoe of Maudite Beer are paddling in mid-air. They watch everything. Most of all, they're watching Thach.

He left Vietnam by boat. He and his wife, their two babies, and a hundred and two other people in a boat no bigger than my living room. He paid a profiteer seventy-five hundred U.S. dollars in gold for the privilege. The trip to Thailand took four days. There was no food. One of the babies almost died.

When they reached their destination, Thai officials took the women and children first. Then a storm came up and overturned the boat, and the men spilled out. Thach managed to catch hold of a rope. He and the other men were in the water for three hours before they were rescued. One man died.

Enter a young woman who lives in the neighbourhood. She isn't buying anything today. She asks Thach how he spells his name. She is a nurse. Thach is going into the hospital soon, to have a lump the size of a walnut removed from his throat. The woman has a friend who nurses at the General, and the friend will look in on Thach.

Thach tells me that his doctor says the lump's benign. He says this like a man who's heard stories about lumps. He knows the way these things can sometimes go. He's scared. You can see it in the way he smiles.

Enter a man with a bag of empty bottles. His hair is grey and wavy and greased. He buys his first beer of the morning. His hands shake. He's working his lips in and out. He needs a drink this morning. He needs it now.

Thach's wife's name is Hoa. They live upstairs. She and Thach take turns in the store from nine in the morning until ten-thirty at night. Hoa says she's been robbed five times. Four times at knifepoint. Once she was threatened with a stick. "The money's not as important as your life," she says.

Hoa tells me she gets tired. Between the house and the store she works sixteen hours a day. "Sometimes," she says, "I get so tired I want to call somebody." There's nobody to call.

Here comes a young man whose jeans look painted on. He has the soft, proud look of a man living with his first girlfriend. At least, I hope that is the look. Otherwise, I have no idea what he's doing buying a box of panty liners.

By the end of the day, the store has grown cold. The door is always opening.

Thach is worried about his throat. So are his wife and sons. There are math lessons to prepare and there's work to do in the store. Thach's wife is tired.

Thach is smiling.

TO HELL WITH THE HABS,
IT'S SOCCER NIGHT IN MONTREAL

A knot of small men with dark faces and flashing smiles slouch in the foyer of the Cégep de Vieux Montreal. They are telling jokes and rolling their eyes, stretching their muscles and slapping their thighs in occasional glee.

They are Latinos, and they are the best soccer players in the city.

Dark women wait on a bench nearby. The cords of their hair are thick and impossibly black. They wear gold hoops in their ears. Their handsome faces are impassive, except when they tend to their babies.

They are here to watch their men play games.

It's better than watching them fight wars.

These are men and women who have known some sorrow and much hard work. You can tell by looking that not all of them have come to Canada by choice. You can tell by looking that none of their children, dressed in clean overalls and bright dresses, will grow up to be soldiers.

A man with a case of pop pushes his way through the crowd. He is followed by two kids carrying plastic sacks, and a young woman with a pair of electric pupusa griddles, and an older woman with a tub of something balanced on her head.

I follow them deep into the belly of the Cégep, where a couple of hundred people—Incas, Mayans, Aztecs—line the bleachers of an enormous gym. Tonight, the Liga Latina-Quebecoise-Tres Americas is wrapping up the indoor soccer season.

The hardwood floor is painted with a dizzy maze of square and parabolic lines for volleyball and basketball, for floor hockey and badminton. There are lines for games I can't imagine, games I'll never play.

Nacional Ecuador in blue strolls out, ready to take on Excelsior, a team of mostly Salvadorans dressed in yellow and black. Play starts with a shrill whistle.

A yellow player dribbles neatly through a crowd and dishes the ball to a mate, who promptly loses it. The dribbler groans, a blue player falls to the floor. The thump of bone on wood is a dull exclamation.

One of the little yellow players makes the ball crawl over his toe, then under his foot and up his heel. He makes it climb behind his back as if it were a mouse in a hurry. He slides it over his shoulder and lets it fall down the front of his chest, dazzling me and his opponent.

But the blue team surges forward, and gets a clear, hard shot. The yellow goalie dives for it. Save! He rolls in mid-air and bounces on the floor—ouf!—but he gives up the rebound. A blue opportunist buries it in the back of the net as if it were a turbot.

Ecuador wins one-zip.

Game Two: Izabal vs. Chinchon Tepek. The Izabal goalie is hugely barrel-chested. He is a bumblebee of a man with spindly legs. He is not meant to fly through the air after balls. The crowd delights in his improbability. He stops every shot.

A poorly-kicked ball flies up and disappears for a moment in the rafters. It falls back down, followed as a lazy afterthought by two badminton birdies which have been nesting up there for who knows how long.

A Chinchon player finally scores, and the crowd cheers and then stops cheering, as if in sympathy for the bumblebee goalie. Chinchon wins, 1-0.

The air smells of pupusas.

Game three is supposed to be Guatemala against El Salvador, but Guatemala is a no-show. The Salvadorans play each other for fun.

I ask the woman next to me how many Latino soccer teams there are in Montreal. She isn't sure. She asks the person sitting next to her. The consensus seems to be eighty teams, with fifteen to twenty players a side.

The players come from Honduras and Peru, Brazil and Nicaragua, El Salvador and Chile, Columbia and Uruguay.

Teams cough up seven hundred and fifty bucks apiece to rent the gym for the indoor season. Each player kicks in two bucks a game to pay the referee. The referees earn their money. A recent game between Peru and Ecuador ended in a brawl.

I eat a pupusa con queso, and a sweet cake.

Now the Peruvian fans wake up. They chant Pay-Roo, Pay-Roo. This game—Juventud Peru against Central of El Salvador—is clearly the one they've come to see. Both sides are evenly matched, but the play is all fits and starts, with more locked arms than a square dance.

But it doesn't sound like square dancing in the stands. Nobody at a square dance shrieks "woo-woo-woo" the way the Peruvian women do. The noise is a cheer or a boo, depending on the circumstances.

When a young Peruvian drills a shot home, a bullet Patrick Roy could not have stopped on his best night, the woo-woos are loud enough to blister paint.

Peru wins.

The last game of the evening is a shoot-out between a team of red Brazilians and some blue Peruvians. It's late at night, and everyone is cranky. The game starts off badly, and deteriorates—two red team-mates begin to shout at each other over a bad play. They wave their fists in each other's faces. The pro-Peruvian crowd loves this kind of stuff, and mocks the pair of them. Woo-woo-woo.

The game carries on up the floor.

At halftime, a pint-sized kid who hopes nobody can see him— you can tell by the furtive look on his face—starts shooting baskets with the soccer ball. His little feet leave the hardwood every time he shoots.

A red Brazilian player rises from the bench and takes the ball from the kid. He dribbles a stylish figure eight, bouncing the ball back and forth between his legs. He's showing off. He sets and shoots. Air ball.

He dribbles around the floor again. The little kid watches with arms folded. The red player weaves once more through imaginary opponents. He sets and shoots again. Air ball again. He shrugs and walks back to the bench.

The little kid picks up the ball, and arcs a mighty two-hander.

And drains it.

In the second half there is a flurry of scoring. El Salvador wins 6-2, more or less. But by now, the crowd is too tired to care about the details. The gym floor clears out quickly. Somebody clambers up on a table and takes down a banner.

Men and boys linger outside the dressing rooms, waiting for brothers, fathers, friends. The women pack up their griddles and go home.

The night sky is black as their hair.

TANGO ON THE MAIN

The modern man-about-town is no boulevardier. He can't afford to be one. He is a single parent and a free lance, he has a couple of jobs and he's got angles on a couple more. He has no time for the old-fashioned life of leisure.

His name is Nantha Kumar.

He's from Malaysia. He's in his mid-thirties, tall and slim and dark, with big brown eyes. He has a walk that's quick and smooth and loping all at once. You've seen him around town.

These days, he's cooking in the kitchen of a watering hole on the Main, the one with the fake surf boards over the bar, the fake palm trees on the floor, and the red pool table in the back. You know the place, even if you don't.

Here is how the modern man-about-town spends his day:

Early morning, a flat in the Plateau. Nantha helps his eight-year old daughter Madhuri get ready for school. His son, Rajiv, is away at camp. The apartment is a cheery mess.

Madhuri is a child with *gravitas*. She eats her breakfast thoughtfully. She combs her hair while Nantha looks for her teddy bear.

On the coffee table is an autobiography of George Orwell. And *Bart Simpson's Guide to Life*. It is a happy combination. Don't have a cow, George.

"What do you do for a living?" asks Madhuri.

She's wearing a white t-shirt and purple stirrup pants. She has a green sock on one foot and a blue sock on the other. I tell her that I write a weekly column in the newspaper. You must work very hard, she says.

Wise child.

Today is Nantha's shopping day. Wednesday, he makes Malay curries. He drops Madhuri off at school, and sets off to find lamb and chicken and shrimp, and more vegetables than you and I can name.

First stop—Chinatown, and breakfast in a little diner. The walls are green, the waiters wear wedge-shaped paper hats. Old grey men sit at the counter telling jokes and smoking cigarettes.

Everyone knows Nantha. He speaks a little Mandarin. He orders a plate of shiu mai and a couple of steamed buns with pork.

A busy morning in the diner. A dozen bowls of rice, topped with chicken feet and sausages, sit in a *bain marie* on the other side of the counter. A waiter hauls a huge roast of beef from the oven. There are half a dozen pots of coffee on the go.

A tiny old woman orders a plate of rice, and points to the beef. The waiter cuts her an inch-thick slice, and flops it on top of the mounded rice. The plateful is nearly as big as she is.

What's the name of this place? No name, says the waiter. How long has it been here? You weren't born yet, says the waiter.

After breakfast, Nantha prowls through Chinatown for lime leaves, fresh turmeric, aubergines, long beans, chives and mustard greens.

And fifty pounds of rice.

Next, we drive uptown to Little Italy, to an Indian store I've never seen before, with shelves of food from Jaffna—southern-style papadums, fresh curry leaves, palm sugar. Nantha speaks their dialect.

On the wall, there is an Indian movie poster with a picture of a barechested gangster standing with his hands on his hips. There is a sneer on his lips and a pistol stuck down the front of his pants. The gangster's girlfriend stands by his side. Her hand is on the pistol. Her finger is on the trigger. She's smiling. He's not.

Nantha speaks their dialect, too.

Last stop is a fish store near the Main. On the way, he lets other drivers cut in front of his van, he stops at zebra crossings, he doesn't sweat the traffic. Parking spaces offer themselves to him wherever he goes.

At the fish store, Nantha eyes a middle-aged Haitian woman. She uses a cane with a brace to help her walk. Nantha whispers something in her ear, makes her laugh, takes her heavy plastic bag of fish and gives it to the scaler.

The woman says Nantha's beautiful. Of course he is. The scaler laughs. Fish scales, delicate as snowflakes, float through the air and fall in a wet mess on the floor.

At noon, Nantha unloads everything at the restaurant, where his right-hand man, Selvan, is preparing the *mise en place.* Selvan is a poet and journalist. He left Sri Lanka when the government shut his paper down. Was he forced to leave?

"I left," he says. "I left."

Nantha prepares a pot of spicy chicken soup, Selvan makes a cup of tea. "Tea from home," he says. "I didn't drink if for two years. The women who pick the tea leaves are indentured. Early in the morning, leeches cling to their legs."

Nantha chops more carrots. He dumps them into a curry of lamb, potatoes, lemon juice. The two men work hard in the narrow galley, passing each other in a fragrant dance. The soup pot boils.

There is no rest for the man about town.

Nantha asks me to slice some of the turmeric. The roots are parchment-coloured and thick as your little finger. Inside, they are pumpkin-coloured. In no time at all, my hands are aglow with bright yellow stain.

Selvan says the women of Sri Lanka use turmeric to dye their faces, hands and feet. They use it as a depilatory. He says they use it once a month to purify themselves.

My hands will remain purified for days.

Nantha has three curries bubbling on the stove—lamb, green chicken, vegetarian. Selvan asks him to head across the street to pick up some dried coconut.

It is no simple trip—every third person stops to chat with Nantha, every fourth person waves from across the street, all the women blow him kisses.

Nantha knows the old lady from Halifax, the one who's hard of hearing. He knows the singer's daughter and the guy in the bicycle helmet. He knows the girl behind the counter of the grocery store, the one who looks like Jessye Norman with a nose ring.

He's got a smile for them all.

Late afternoon: Elaine comes into the bar, sits down at a table and unwraps a block of cheese. Nantha joins her. There is some talk of tango. Nantha loads a tape in the stereo and leads her onto the floor.

Elaine wears a short and clingy purple dress. She wears black stockings. Two Portuguese men drinking beer at the bar watch her feet make the intricate steps. No, they don't.

They watch her legs.

She leaves, Nantha goes back to the kitchen. The student crowd drifts in for glasses of happy-hour beer, for chicken wings and chips. He speaks their dialect.

And then the people in the know, the ones who've been to Malaysia, drift in for satay, for fried noodles and plates of curry. Everyone knows Nantha. Maybe he is a boulevardier, after all.

Smart enough to make the boulevard come to him.

HALF-TON MONSTERS HAULING DREAMS
AROUND AN OVAL TRACK

Jack Calce is a horse trainer. He is a young man with a gee-golly grin, a ruddy complexion and a purple scar in the middle of his forehead, where he was kicked last week by a two-year-old colt named Digger.

Jack was trimming Digger's mane. The horse was frightened by the electric buzz of the clippers, and reared up on its hind legs.

Jack says he didn't feel a thing. He says he clutched his head, took five steps to the side, wobbled and tripped on a pitch fork, then fell over on the floor.

Six stitches.

Some days, the horse trains you.

Jack's girlfriend Tamara scrunches her mouth and rolls her eyes, as if to say she knows it hurt like hell. Tamara's dark, shoulder-length hair is pulled off her face and pinned high behind her head. She and Jack are in their twenties, and they're head over heels in love. With each other and with horses.

Jack trains a stable of eight, four of which—Sentaza, Caracalla, Licorice Star and the horse with the sharp hoof—belong to Maurice Pagé.

Pagé used to be in cattle. He had a hundred and twenty head of pure-bred Charolais. Then he had three operations on his hips.

Now Pagé, his trainer and his trainer's girl are sitting in a barn at Blue Bonnets, in a tiny office near the stalls, chasing the morning chill with coffee and doughnuts and dreams.

They are telling stories of Sentaza, the queen of the stable, fresh off a twenty-two hundred dollar purse. You'd almost think the filly knows she is a winner. There is an awareness to the way she holds her head.

Pagé says, "You should have seen her run. She was running smooth. You could have put that cup of coffee on her back, it wouldn't have fallen off." He twirls his waxed moustache. The morning light glints off his gold rings.

There is a sweet smell in the air, the smell of straw and horse shit, cedar oil and hoof cream, iodines and lotions. The barn cat hops up on the table and sniffs the bag of doughnuts. Jack stubs out his cigarette, and starts to muck the stalls.

Outside, orange banners snap in the wind, and dull brown sparrows peck for grain in the dust at the edge of the track, oblivious to the hard hooves flying by their heads.

The horses are trotters and pacers. You know the difference. A trotter runs the way a soldier marches—left right left. A pacer zunts—both rights, then both lefts.

Either way, it's a pretty sight.

Some horses jog, some run to feel their muscles, and some run flat out, with their dark manes flying. Their drivers sit behind them, perched on sulkies. Each driver holds hard-bitten hope, along with a stop-watch in one hand and a five-foot whip in the other.

It's a risky business. A half-ton horse is a delicate monster, capable of breaking its leg or bowing a tendon or dropping dead like that from who knows what.

When Jack is done mucking the stalls, Tamara helps him get Dream Warrior ready for his run. She fits the five-year old stud with halter and harness and the hopples—pronounced hobbles—which keep his legs gaited when he runs.

Dream Warrior also takes an overcheck to keep his head high, and a head pole with a burr, to keep him running straight—what a horse should have he did not lack, save a proud rider on so proud a back.

Instead, sitting lightly in the sulky, he has Jack.

And after a couple of brisk turns round the track, the little trainer with the scar on his brow unhitches the horse and washes him down with a bucket of soapy water.

Jack was born in Montreal, but he grew up in Saratoga Springs. He fell for horses there, and went to a school for trainers. He learned the finer points of brushing—with the grain, not against—plus walking, bathing, wrapping of legs, lameness, anatomy, how to pick out a hoof, and how to take care of harness and bridle parts.

If you think that's easy, a simple little halter consists of a brow band, an upper check bit, a lower check bit, a crown, two blinds, a snaffle bit, a nose band, a throat latch and a bunch of other bits and pieces I forget.

Back in the office, the barn cat with the nose for doughnuts hops up on the window ledge, staring at dust motes in the light, or whatever it is cats stare at. Jack finishes a cigarette.

The cat's tail twitches, and with a flip of her right paw so fast you can't see it, she bats an empty pop can off the window ledge. The pop can flies through the air and skitters over the floor. The cat is still as a statue, as if nothing happened. Jack tosses the can in the garbage.

Caracalla and Digger are the last two horses of the day. Jack takes one, Maurice takes the other. The horses jog around the back track, running one-two, pulling lightly. The hopples slap, the sulkies squeak, you can hear the clop of the hooves. They disappear around the far turn.

In the distance, a red kite swoops in the air. A yellow plane flies overhead, an orange CP engine lumbers by. And now the horses come flying down the stretch, part kite, part locomotive. Their hooves dig in, the wheels of the sulkies are a blur. I can hear the animals breathing.

Jack's face is flecked white with horse spit and dust.

He washes his face, and hoses down the horses. Then he and Tamara wrap legs and slap heel cream on hooves. I tell them there's a place near my house that serves horse meat with french fries. It is a conversation stopper.

The horses fuss in their stalls.

It's time for their buckets of feed. Jack gives them a mixture of bran and corn, oats, molasses and vitamins, very nearly what I had for breakfast. Stormy Lad kicks his stall as he eats. The barn cat falls asleep on the table in the office, curled up next to the doughnuts.

Jack's horses aren't racing tonight.

There will be no winners, but no losers either, no bowed tendons or broken legs or any of the hundred other things that can go wrong when a delicate, half-ton monster hurries a dream around an oval track.

The Diamond as Big as the Ritz Makes the Bed

Jackie Roy, chambermaid, approaches the first room of her day. She pauses for a moment and takes a deep breath. If you have ever slept in a hotel—any hotel, not just the Ritz, where Jackie works—you know this is a moment which requires discretion.

On both sides of the door.

She knocks three times. There is no answer. She puts the key in the lock, and opens the door a crack. She looks down at the floor. She does not wish to see what she should not.

No one likes surprises.

"Hello," she asks, "can I disturb you?"

She has a firm, clear voice. She opens the door six inches more and advances a single step, still looking down. She fiddles with her keys and knocks again on the open door. "Hello, can I disturb you?" There is no response. The room is free.

And Jackie Roy begins to work.

She moves quickly, with the nervousness of a hummingbird. She is five feet tall, she weighs all of eighty pounds, and her hair is permed in a style and colour reminiscent of that worn by your mother's best friend.

The one who still smokes.

The first thing Jackie does is strip the bed. Then she gathers up the towels from the bathroom. She straightens the shelf of toiletries near the mirror. She turns on the tap in the tub, then cleans the sink and kneels in front of the toilet and scrubs that, too.

She gives the floor a swab by hand. The bathroom takes her less than twenty minutes, and it sparkles top to bottom. I am already tired, but she has just begun.

She places a clean bottom sheet at the centre of the foot of the bed and flips it forward. She takes the top corners of the sheet to the head of the bed. She gives all four corners a hospital tuck. Her hands are deft and quick, precise.

By the time she finishes, she has circled the bed fifteen times from one side to the other, adding a second sheet, a blanket, a top sheet, pillows and a bedspread. She smooths the bedspread with the flat of her hand and tucks it under the pillows with two short chops.

She cleans fourteen rooms a day. She works five days a week. You figure out how many sheets she smooths, corners she tucks, and pillows she chops in the course of the year. The dignity of labour rests not in the work, but in the honest worker.

In our house we sleep under a duvet.

Still, there are days when our bed does not get done. Today is one of those days. I feel slightly guilty as I watch her work.

I ask Jackie if she made her own bed this morning. I am prepared to forgive her if she has not. She gives me a look. It is one of those looks, as if she is wondering what kind of wise guy I am.

Mme. Jackie Roy draws herself up and says, "I did the laundry. And I made the bed. Before I came to work." And I am the one who should be forgiven. Jackie forgives me easily. She shows me the Royal Suite.

She leads me through it casually, as if it is no big deal. It is a big deal. It has a sauna and an office with plush leather chairs and a massive pedestal desk. Sophia Loren made spaghetti sauce in the little kitchen. The Queen Mother slept in the four-poster bed.

Here, Jackie has taken care of the actress Bujold and the singer Ferland. Here, Michael Jackson watched the television which is hidden discreetly in an ancient Chinese lacquer television stand. Jackie sniffs. "He slept all day." It's hard to clean a room when guests do that. "This," says Jackie, "is a three hour room."

And so it goes, without let-up, until lunch. Jackie eats with the rest of the hotel staff in the diner in the basement of the hotel. Like many tiny people, she packs a big plate. Like many smokers, she eats quickly and then lights up.

In the third room after lunch, there is a response to her knock. A guest is still in his room, watching a movie on TV. People who can afford the Ritz are not like you and me. Sometimes they stay in their rooms all day. For whatever reason.

Jackie enters cautiously.

She asks the man how he likes the weather, and sets about the business of cleaning up his room. He nods at the television while she works and says, "Quite an actor, Dee Par Doo."

"What's that?" says Jackie as she carries out his sheets.

"Dee Par Doo," says the guest. "He's quite an actor."

Jackie says, "Oh, yes." She has no idea what the man is talking about. She finishes the room quickly and leaves.

We head for the supply room where the towels are stored. Jackie gets us room-service coffees. She lights up a smoke and tells me chambermaid stories.

She says eastern potentates always call for a valet to pack and unpack their bags. She says once she brought flowers from her own home for that nice Patsy Gallant. She says most people don't tip the chambermaid, but the Chinese always do; they leave their tips in envelopes under the pillow.

Has she ever found anything valuable left in a room, after a guest has checked out? "Oh, yes. You would be surprised," she says. What does she do if she finds something of value?

She turns it over to Housekeeping, where it is tagged with the date and the time it was found, the name of the person who used the room, and the name of the chambermaid. If the item is not claimed after a certain amount of time, it is given to the chambermaid who found it.

Why won't the hotel call you if you forget something of value?

Ah, this is a matter of discretion.

Suppose the maid finds a black silk scarf in the room after you have checked out. Suppose the hotel calls your home and your wife, who does not own a black silk scarf, answers the phone.

You see the problem.

Over the years, Jackie of the Ritz has claimed a 35 mm camera, a pair of silver earrings and a gold bracelet. "A good one," she says, "made of rose gold. I gave it to my daughter."

Jackie stubs out her cigarette, takes a deep breath, and hauls her housekeeping truck back to work. She performs the same set of tasks the same way day after day. It is almost a relief, a break in the routine, when she calls for the hotel plumber to unclog the drain in a tub.

In the last room of the day, a guest has placed a bag of fruit on a table near the bed. Jackie purses her lips and says, "The poor man. I'll be right back."

She returns with a plate, a napkin and some silver. She brings a finger bowl, and rests it on a doily. She arranges the grapes, the apples and the banana with a practised hand. She lays out the cutlery. Then Jackie Roy steps back to see if everything is correct. Of course it is.

And the diamond as big as the Ritz calls it a day.

SUCH A KIDDER

He is sitting by himself at a table in a dark little comedy club, deep in the belly of a downtown hotel. There are mirrors on the ceiling, mirrors behind the bar, mirrors along one wall. When Ernie Butler laughs, a reflected crowd roars.

Butler owns the Comedy Nest. It is late in the afternoon. He is listening to three singing comics audition. At this hour, any light that penetrates the club ricochets from the ashtrays on the tables to the chrome edges of the chairs and back again.

Dreams splinter easily on hard surfaces, but these kids are energetic and loopy enough that even Belafonte would laugh at their macabre version of "The Banana Boat Song."

Six foot, seven foot, eight foot corpse.
Come, Mr. Undertaker, bury me cadaver.

Butler seems genuinely amused. Hope lives for one more afternoon. He promises the kids he'll call them soon. You get the impression he means it.

If only the evening held as much hope.

A group of social workers and social work volunteers is trickling into the club for an evening of Comedy With A Cause. This is Butler's pet project, a way to keep the club full and the comics working, while at the same time raising money for worthy causes.

Tonight, he is apprehensive. Social work isn't funny. The tables are filling with an assortment of earnest young people and white-haired older folk. This is not your drink-swilling, thigh-slapping crowd.

One of the comics patrols the back of the room with a tight grin on his face, and one last cigarette in his fist. He has the look of a man who would smash himself in the face with a brick if that would get a laugh.

Tonight, he may need that brick.

Suddenly, the lights go out. There is a familiar and ear-splitting fanfare over the speakers, and a cartoon spills onto the big white screen behind the stage. It is a triple-header featuring Elmer, Daffy and Bugs. Elmer hunts in the woods. Bugs makes wisecracks. Daffy runs his mouth until Elmer shoots his beak off.

Th-th-that's all, folks.

If comedy is a science, this room is as exciting as a chemistry lab. The social workers seem uptight, unsure about laughing in each other's company. It will take more than a wascally wabbit to bring this house down.

Ernie Butler is more than a wascally wabbit.

As the cartoon ends, he bounds on stage like a Tasmanian devil and immediately hurls a naughty joke. He is probing the outer limits of the house, on the look-out for taboos. If anybody's going to bomb tonight, better it be him.

But he is too wacky, too frenetic and too rude to bomb. Soon the jokes are falling like hapless dominoes and the social workers are laughing, in spite of themselves, out of the palm of his hand.

Now, his work done, Butler hands over the house to his comedians; one after another, they are free to step forward, take the mike and reap the benefits of his generosity. Punch-lines begin to spray the room like bullets from a machine gun:

I tried to move in with my parents. But they'd just moved in with their parents. Ba-da-boom. *I had a sweater. It fit like a glove. It had five sleeves.* Ba-da-boom.

The crowd howls, and Butler prowls the room while the comedians dig up funny bones. Now he's backstage, now he's at the bar with a diet pop and a cigarette, dropping a word in a nervous comic's ear, listening to the audience, greeting a friend, telling a private joke of his own.

There was a time when his glass was full of harder stuff than pop. There was a time you couldn't get him to listen. Butler's been listening carefully for a year and a half now. He's getting good at it.

His ears prick up before anyone else's do—one of the comics begins to die a slow and painful death on stage. He's seen it coming. It hurts. The social workers squirm audibly in their seats, even though they've been trained to be polite and show approval to anyone making an honest effort.

Butler watches calmly. The woman's on her own. Anything that does not kill her will make her stronger. Hey, it could be worse—at a comedy club long ago, he saw a customer bean a comic with an ashtray. The comic leapt into the crowd and thrashed his critic to a pulp.

None of that tonight. The woman limps away painfully. Her only wounds are self-inflicted. Butler jumps back on stage and picks up the mood like a manic weightlifter. He turns the crowd easily. No sweat. His day has been spent on errands more difficult, more important than this.

He put in an hour with his kids at the day care centre, helping his seven-year-old son with his spelling, reading his five-year-old daughter a story. He even peeked in at a group of toddlers lined up against a wall in their high-chairs. He made faces at them till he got a laugh. If he can get a response there, he can get one here.

By the time Heidi Foss takes the stage, a gut-busting balance has been restored. Dressed in black, she is a handsome woman with an air of deadpan deviltry.

She cocks her head and looks off to the side. *"My shrink thinks I'm a kleptomaniac. He wouldn't say it to my face. I read it in his notebook when I got home."* Ba-da-boom. *"I bought a police dog. Not for protection. I needed help to find my drugs."* Ba-da-boom. The helping professions are chuckling again.

They eat up every separatist joke tossed in their laps. *Quebeckers can move out of Canada,* says David John McCarthey, *but they won't get their security deposit back—there are beer cans and cigarette butts all over the place.* Ba-da-boom.

At the end of the evening, the head social worker gets on stage, draws names from a hat, hands out prizes to the volunteers. They've made some bucks, they've had some yuks. They're happy as they can be.

Butler sits in his chair, exhausted.

"Look," he says, "this is hard work. I'm a 47-year-old man. " In the mirrors surrounding the club, he looks older than that. He's been leading the nightlife since he was 16. There are as many stories of Butler the heller as there are jokes about booze or dope.

Now his idea of the nightlife includes forty winks in an apartment near The Nest, where there are pictures of his kids in the living room, and a pile of his daughter's teddy bears on the bed. "I'm not a very interesting guy right now," he sighs.

That Ernie.

Such a kidder.

DOG DAY AFTERNOON

Let the dogs bark until they are hoarse. George—he is a veterinarian's cat, orange and white, superior to his kind and contemptuous of all others—sleeps where he wants, and wanders where he will.

If he could speak as he strolls past the closed kennels, he'd say: "My master is the master over all of you, but I am master over him." Master, that is, over Dr. Don Floyd of the Baker Animal Hospital.

Morning rounds: Dr. Floyd looks in on a dog named Ittak, a Canadian Eskimo dog from Iqaluit. The dog is recovering from an operation. A kid in Iqaluit threw him a ball. Ittak ate it. Dr. Floyd had to operate.

Today's patients include a scrawny house cat which is growing old, and seems unwilling to groom itself. There is a Corgi requiring shots, and a Dalmatian with an infected ear and a host of allergies.

A woman follows, out of breath, in the wake of three wildly mismatched dogs: a miniature poodle which might have been knitted from white wool, a Wheaton Terrier with an intelligent, square head, and a nervous whippet-shepherd cross.

The whippet is a long lean line from nose to tail; it could slip through the eye of a needle if it had to, and looks as if it would like nothing better. The poodle's name is Timex; he yips and trips all over himself and everything in his path.

Why is the poodle called Timex? "I wanted a watch dog." I see. "We were going to call him Rolex, but we didn't want him stolen." Oh. "Ha aha aha," say her three dogs, their pink tongues hanging out of their mouths.

While Dr. Floyd sees the rest of the day's patients, his colleague, Dr. Raemona Slodovnik, dresses for surgery. Her cap is blue, her mask is pink, her gown is the colour of water-washed ink. She has her work cut out for her today—a cat spay, and a pair of dog castrations.

First up is the kitty, lying on its back on the operating table in an anaesthetic stupor. Slodovnik begins with a neat incision low on kitty's belly. Her hand is sure. She's done this thousands of times.

She widens the sharp red wound, cutting through layers of fat and muscle. She pokes into the meat of the belly with a hooked instrument and pulls up a stringy pink bit. Here, inside the living envelope, is the uterine horn.

Kitty breathes in slowly. My stomach clenches, as if it were filled with ice. The back of my neck begins to prickle. I have to leave and catch my breath.

While I am gone, Slodovnik isolates and cuts the ovary, then hauls up the second horn and ties, and cuts. Finally, she removes the uterus completely. It looks like a V about four inches long, with little pink beans at the upper points.

She discards it, and closes.

Castrations are simpler. A buff-colored Keeshond named Baron lies on his back, his glory shaved and exposed for all to see. Dr. Slodovnik cuts through the scrotum with a scalpel. Out pops a testicle. Mine rise perceptibly. Slodovnik ties, cuts, discards, and sews: where once Baron was proudly round, bulging with male plenitude, now he is flat and impotent.

She performs the same procedure on a muscular young Doberman. The flesh of the bigger dog seems somehow redder; its wound looks like a bitten plum. A Doberman's are the size of walnuts. Dogs know nothing of irony—Slodovnik sews the incision with catgut.

The Doberman will awake not knowing what he lacks. In years ahead he may feel a residual hormonal tug; he will hear a litter of never-born puppies, calling to him across a chasm in a doggy dream.

Meanwhile, Dr. Floyd is taking care of an anaesthetized Brittany Spaniel with a dislocated hip. X-rays show the ball of the joint, floating free of the socket. Floyd pulls and twists the leg with all his might. Every time the joint pops in, it pops back out again.

The vet leans and pulls harder, and the unconscious dog voids. Floyd cleans it up, and leans again on Rocky's hip, pushing and pulling at the same time. Rocky voids again. Floyd cleans it up again.

After half an hour of work, Floyd has exhausted himself and all his options. He has to operate. In short order, Rocky's hip is shaved and disinfected, and Dr. Floyd draws a scalpel over the skin.

It is a curious operation. He cuts deeply and smoothly as far as the ball of the hip, and frees it from the surrounding flesh; the procedure is not unfamiliar to anyone who has ever boned a turkey—you part the meat, you free the bone.

Deep in an anarchy of wet, red flesh, the ball joint gleams dully. Floyd taps at it four times, sharply, like a sculptor with chisel and hammer. He severs the top of the joint from the bone, as if it were a malignant bud of the tip of a green twig. Floyd cleans up the flesh and sews it back together, layer by layer, until the wound is closed.

The cut bone and the socket will eventually form a false joint, allowing Rocky pretty much the same freedom he had before. The procedure will cost his owner close to four hundred bucks. Rocky will have a sore hip when he wakes up.

He will not be able to stand for a few days, but he should be walking normally in a couple of months. For the moment he lies on his side, unconscious. George, the veterinarian's cat, stares at him and sniffs.

MILO'S GLASSES

Milo Bosner is seven years old, and today is the lousiest day of his life. He's in the first grade, he's a little out of step, and he has to get a pair of geeky glasses. He's feeling just a little glum in his yellow raincoat and his rubber boots. But I wouldn't worry about him too much.

Milo is a puppet. He was constructed in part from the childhood experience of the elegantly bespectacled young animator, Brian Duchscherer.

Milo's the star of "Glasses," an NFB short about love and mortality in grade one. It's a story about the dangers of growing up without a sense of humour. It's a story about a boy who finds out who his true friends are.

Today, Milo begins his day face down on a prairie road. It's been raining, he's been tripped, and he's lost his lunch pail. Remember what that's like?

It's a key scene in the film.

Animation is tedious—Duchscherer will shoot fifty frames of film today, one frame at a time. Prior to each shot, he will adjust and readjust the puppet's hand or foot or elbow, trying to get the movement right. At twenty-four frames a second, he'll finish the day with two seconds' worth of film.

The camera Brian uses is old and black, and the film goes into a contraption on top which looks like a pair of mouseketeer's ears. Apt, when you consider that every time he shoots a frame, the film advances with an "eep" of sound, as if the camera really were a mouse and Brian was stepping on its tail.

In this sequence, Milo raises his head. Eep! He looks up. Eep! He looks down at the pavement where he's fallen. Eep! He looks up once again. Eep! He rises on one knee and then springs forward, chasing his friend Gwenny down the road.

Eep, eep, eep.

Brian adjusts the orbit of Milo's eyes with a little needle every time the puppet moves. I flinch at this. Over on the workbench, there's a little box of Milo heads with open-mouthed expressions, and I see a paper card stuck with eight little pairs of Gwenny eyeballs. It's creepy to look at.

When "Glasses" is finally finished, it will cost between three and four hundred thousand dollars. Eep! Hey, in the world of animated film, that's cheap.

While Milo's on centre stage, with a little wooden grain silo, some twig trees and a cloudy, spray-painted prairie sky in the background, Gwenny and I share a seat.

She's a foot high, she weighs just a bit more than a pound. Her skin is rubbery, her fingers move independently, and with the tiny eyeballs she's wearing today, she looks wise beyond her years.

She's dressed in a hot pink raincoat and a pink sou'wester. She has no scenes today. She nestles into the crook of my arm while we watch Milo work.

Around us, out of the bright lights, there is a confusion of boxes, rolls of tape, spray bottles, glues and scissors, empty pop cans, projector bulbs and flesh-coloured puppet body parts. I begin to feel protective of Gwenny in the midst of all the chaos, as if...oh, for pete's sake, get a grip.

You see what I mean. Puppets have personalities of their own. Brian says some days they seem to move by themselves. He ought to know. He built them all by hand, milling their little joints from brass and aluminum, and casting their little rubber heads. At least they don't demand little puppet lunches.

Animators do.

On our way to the Film Board cafeteria, we pass an Oscar in a display case. It seems dusty and a little cheap, as if it had been bought off the shelf at "Oscars 'R Us." Oscars aren't what they used to be, says Brian—the older ones are thicker-plated, they seem to have more weight.

Hmm. The man knows film.

The corridors of the NFB are wide, the walls are thick and the colours are beige and grey. It looks oddly dull for a creative shop. There is also a peculiar smell about the place, which could come from the chemicals used for processing film.

But it's possible the smell is the odour of cutbacks, and the dullness a residual of the funk exuded by some of the staff trying to decide if they should take early retirement from the work they love, while other staff look to the future and wonder if they were right to start working here at all.

Duchscherer's on contract.

The funk in the halls extends to the cafeteria. I take a sandwich marked "chicken," but I can't honestly tell what's inside. It could be tuna. It could be eggs. It could be soylent green. It has no taste whatsoever.

The only thing that's animated here are the animators.

One of the women sitting at our table begins to tell the story of two of her neighbours who got into a fight on the street the other night. One neighbour had a baseball bat, and the other was armed with a broomstick. There was much yelling and waving of weapons, but no damage in the end.

It sounds like the script for an NFB short.

"Glasses" will be released next spring. It will run twelve minutes. It's one of those films you probably should have seen when you were six. It's one of those films you should see if you wear glasses or if you have kids.

How closely does art imitate life?

Milo and Brian both got glasses in the first grade. They both have great big slate-blue eyes. They share a certain vulnerability, a sense that the world is somehow not as sweet a place as it ought to be, as it used to be.

There are a lot of people at the NFB who'd agree.

MARINO'S PUMP

He wouldn't say much on the phone. He said he had what I wanted, and asked if I was still interested. I said I was. We agreed to meet. He gave me some instructions, and told me where and how to find him.

The whole thing sounded hush-hush. I wasn't sure what I was getting into. I took the métro one stop further than I had to, then I doubled back.

Actually, I missed my stop. Still, you can't be too careful in this business. Never mind. It worked. There was no one on my tail.

That was only half the battle.

We were supposed to meet at a coffee shop in a mall in the east end, but when I came up from the métro, I couldn't find the entrance to the mall. I'd make a lousy spy. I have no sense of direction. I stumbled around in the falling snow. Finally, I got my bearings and found the door.

I might not have a sense of direction, but I am a good judge of character. I spotted him right away. He looked like he was waiting.

John Marino is fifty-five years old. He's an electrician. He used to repair elevators for a living—not a bad job for a guy who flunked the seventh grade a couple of times and then dropped out of school.

He's retired now. He sent me a letter and some drawings a while ago. Said he'd designed a hydraulic pump capable of creating clean energy from the movement of the ocean. He told me he'd built a prototype.

That's what I wanted to see.

We shook hands in the lobby of the mall. He escorted me down a hall, then up some stairs. We stopped in front of a little office. It was Saturday. The office was empty. Marino pushed open the door. And there it was.

The Helical Hydraulic Pump.

It was sitting in a case on the reception desk.

I peered at it.

The case looked like a lunch box. The helical part of the pump looked like a curly french fry, except it's made of plastic tubing and it's wrapped around an armature, and the armature is powered by ratchets which can be driven by the action of pontoons floating on the water.

When the curly french-fry tubing rotates, it's supposed to scoop up water through the open end. Water flows inside the curliness and is somehow forced up a vertical column into a storage tank. I say somehow. It's not an Archimedes screw, but it's not unlike one, either.

Marino wants to give me an immediate demonstration. "No, wait," I tell him, "let's talk first." "No" he insists, "let me show you how it works." I give in. He's a big guy. I step back.

He hooks up the vertical column to the back of the lunch pail, attaches some tubes. The lunch pail thing is already full of dirty-looking water. I think he was practising while he waited for me.

Now Marino rotates the armature with a socket wrench. And lo! Water passes down the curly tube, just like he said it would. Water climbs up the column, and fills the storage tank at the top of the column, just like he said it would; and when it reaches a certain pressure, the water gushes out.

Enough water to power a tiny turbine.

Just like he said.

Simple, huh? Too simple. So simple, Marino can't get anyone to take him seriously. What do I know about these things? I'm no engineer. I can barely change a tap washer. But it looks like it works to me.

We sit down to talk.

I can understand his earlier reluctance. Marino's grown tired of talking, tired of persuading, tired of begging people to listen. Even the guys he plays poker with figure he should just shut up and forget about it. On the other hand, maybe they're just cheesed off because he took them for eighty bucks last week. Never mind.

I ask him if he's had any luck getting patents. He rolls his eyes. He shows me documents. He's been given the run-around in Quebec, and the run-around in Ottawa. He's been brushed off by ministers of government, by bureaucrats and flacks; he's been treated like a fool.

He picks up a sheaf of official-looking letters. I notice he has huge hands; they are calloused and stained, the hands of a working man. The letters all say the same thing: *this pump will never work; it's too simple to work; we've seen stuff like this that didn't work; it's obvious to us this pump doesn't work.*

Yes, well, what do I know, but it looks like it works to me. It's based on existing technology—an Italian guy patented something similar in 1872. The Americans, who aren't averse to entrepreneurial spirit, and who know a good thing when they see one, gave Marino a patent on the pump last year.

But he's still frustrated. He's convinced his invention could be a source of energy so efficient Hydro Quebec would never have to flood any land, never have to build any more dams, never have to foul up the environment.

But nobody will take him seriously. What's he going to do? He doesn't know. He ain't slick. He's not an engineer. Marino sighs.

He's an ordinary guy who had the bad luck to be seized with a good idea. He's twenty thousand dollars out of pocket. He's frustrated. He says it's not the money. He believes in the device. I tell him he looks hurt by the fact that no one's taking him seriously. He says, "You're not wrong."

It's too bad, really.

Marino's just the sort of name you'd want for a guy who is convinced he can harvest energy from the oceans.

ALEXANDER GRAHAM BELL
ROLLED OVER IN HIS GRAVE

The other night, I called one of those telepersonal services. The kind where you meet people just like yourself over the phone. For intimate conversations. Or just for fun. I wanted to know who was out there and what they were saying. I wanted to know who was reaching out and touching someone.

There isn't much touching. You call and leave a message for someone, they call and leave a message for you. And so on, ad infinitum. Press one to return to the main menu. Press pound for more options.

It turns out the telepersonals are a form of voice-mail telephone tag with a bunch of people you've never met, some of whom have no clothes on.

If you believe them, that is.

It takes money to enter the system. For ten bucks, you get five minutes of time. This is the special introductory rate. After that, you can buy an hour for $36, two and a half hours for $72, or six hours for a $140. As the operator says, that's just 39¢ a minute.

As the operator also says, women call free. And for men, if there are no women on the line, there is no charge. Are you getting a glimmer about the set-up?

I took the plunge anyway.

In the name of research, dammit.

I recorded my name on the voice mail system. Then I recorded a description of myself. If you must know, I added an inch in height and subtracted twenty pounds. Then the voice mail voice asked me to record what I was wearing.

A suit of armour and snowshoes.

The voice asked if I wanted to let other members listen in on my calls. They call it peeping.

I don't think so.

Have you ever written a description of yourself for a personal ad? Try coming up with one live, on the spot, over the phone. It's embarrassing. It took me half a dozen tries to get my messages recorded.

Once you're in the system, other people can listen to your description and leave messages for you. That's when the telephone tag begins. It's a sad game. Everybody's surfing in the system, looking for somebody right.

And if nobody wants to talk to you, tough luck.

The Voice of Interactive Communications says it takes no responsibility for the physical or mental health of the callers, and advises caution when dating someone new. Always good advice.

New caller. Angela, age twenty-two. Brown hair, blue eyes. Five feet, five inches. She describes herself as open-minded. She says she's listening to Aerosmith.

I'm too old for this.

The Voice advises there are ten women and five men on the line.

New caller. Georgie is attractive, outgoing, five foot three, athletic, blonde hair, green eyes, warm and adventurous, sexy, passionate and sensual. I send her a couple of messages. The voice mail says she's busy. I'm not surprised.

The Voice says there is a message for me. Human contact at last. Somebody belches into my ear. Same to you, jerk.

Again, The Voice asks if I want to let others peep in on my calls. I don't think so.

The Voice says I have a message. Kelly is forty-two. We start to talk. She's not working. She's a short order cook. She broke up with her boyfriend last year. Her daughter thought it would be good therapy for her to call the telepersonals.

Kelly says she went out with a guy she met over the phone. He came to her house and took off his boots and put his feet on the table and said he wanted sex.

She excused herself and went to the phone in the kitchen. She called her daughter, who showed up two minutes later with ten friends.

I told Kelly to be careful about who she takes home.

Ten p.m. Most of the members on the line are women between the ages of eighteen and twenty-two. They all seem to be mostly five foot two. I leave a number of messages. No response at all.

I'm beginning to take it personally.

At ten-thirty, I get a call from Sarah. She has a nice voice. She quickly initiates an X-rated conversation. I deflect it, and we chat about other things. She's fifty years old. She has asthma. She needs to lose a hundred pounds. She can't work outside her house.

She tells me she's just started to make a living talking dirty on the phone. She's using the telepersonals to practise. She can't find any other way to make any money. She left her husband last year. A year ago, she didn't even know there was such a thing a dirty phone calls.

I wished her luck.

Eleven thirty-five. Once again, The Voice asks if I'll let other members peep in on my calls. I don't think so. Then I get a frantic call from a woman with a low and husky voice. I call back. We get connected. After a minute, it becomes apparent that the caller is a man.

Oh, yuck.

The Voice says there are twelve women and six men on the line. Tonight it's also clear there are several hookers who want to talk. They leave breathy messages describing big these and hot those. I get a couple of professional-sounding offers to meet.

I don't think so.

Two a.m. New caller on the line. Sophie is thirty-two. She's half Italian and half Polish. Canada is her third country in the past three years. She hates it here. No first-class art, no first-class music, no first-class clothes. Nothing here but money and sex.

My ear is sore.

She was engaged to be married. A month before the wedding, she learned her boyfriend was sleeping with three or four other women. Better to find this out a month before the wedding than a month after, she says.

And so it goes. There are teenaged girls who just want to talk. And professional talkers whose role is to keep the men talking on the phone. There are hookers, and women whose marriages have gone bust. There are some strange and lonely men. We are an odd mixture of truth and lies and longing.

The Voice says I've come to the end of the member listing.

THE COLD LIFE OF A MONTREALER IN THE ARCTIC

Sometimes people go North because they love the way of life. Sometimes they go North because they love the money. Sometimes they go because they don't fit in down south. The North is big enough to take these people in.

But sometimes lives blow up, and the North is where the pieces fall. This is the story of Marcel N. of Montreal. His life blew up. He landed in Inuvik.

Look on your map of Canada, up in the top left corner. Inuvik is as far away from Montreal as you can get.

Marcel repairs industrial refrigeration equipment for a living. You might find that funny—how much work can there be for a refrigerator man in a town that's cold as a landlord's heart for nine months of the year?

But this is not a funny story.

One night last summer, Marcel came home from work and his wife of thirteen years said she didn't love him any more. That's what she said. She hadn't loved him for a year. And she kicked him out of the house.

Marcel was stunned.

He had no idea there were any problems. He doesn't do drugs or drink or smoke. He never laid a hand on her in anger. He never ran around.

He shakes his head. "All I took when I left was my laundry and my jacket." And his broken heart. "I miss my kids," he says. "I love my kids."

Marcel and I are having coffee, a couple of Montrealers killing time on a Saturday afternoon in Inuvik. We are sitting in the lounge of the Mackenzie Hotel. On Mackenzie Road. Down the street from Sir Alexander Mackenzie School.

It's a small town.

Michelle the waitress is making herself busy behind the bar. She's a big girl with a tattoo on her shoulder. She looks everywhere except at us, a sure sign that she's listening hard. The North is full of stories.

A month after Marcel moved out, he says, "There was another guy in my house. A young guy from Romania. Sleeping in my bed. Living with my kids."

Michelle winces; that's a tough one, even in the North.

Marcel's son, André, is nine years old and his daughter Suzanne is six. He shows me the photo-studio picture he keeps in his wallet. Suzanne is wearing a red dress. André wears a white shirt buttoned at the collar. Cute kids.

Marcel moved into his mother's house when his wife kicked him out. But a man can't live with his mother. Last September, he noticed an ad at the Manpower office—refrigerator man wanted in Inuvik.

What the hell.

He applied for the job, even though he didn't speak a word of English. Nor a word of Gwich'in or Inuvialuktun, the other languages of Inuvik. No matter. With the help of translators at both ends of the call, Marcel was offered the job.

Refrigeration is its own language.

He had no idea where Inuvik was.

He'd never seen it on the map. He asked the stewardess on the plane to Calgary if she knew where Inuvik was. "North of here," she said. He asked the stewardess on the plane from Calgary to Norman Wells, and from Norman Wells to Yellowknife.

"North of here." they said.

Let me tell you about Inuvik.

Last week in Inuvik it was forty-one below. You can get the *Globe & Mail,* weather permitting, every afternoon. It will cost you a buck seventy-five.

You can go to the Northern Store and buy a piece of lynx trim for your parka. You can buy a pound of butter and a rifle. You can buy a ghetto blaster and a frying pan.

You better bring your wallet.

It's expensive.

If you spill your coffee in the snow—and anything spilled freezes quickly these days—big black ravens will come along and peck it up in jagged chunks.

In Inuvik for fun on the weekend, you drink at the Zoo or the Mad Trapper. That's fine if you drink. Marcel doesn't like to drink.

What kind of life does he have?

He shares a house with another worker. He's learned English quickly, but he's aching to hear French. He's trying hard to make friends. He's lonely.

After thirteen years of marriage, he's a tentative bachelor. "There are two kinds of girls in Inuvik," Marcel says. "Drunk or married. The good ones are married. The other ones are drunk."

Marcel asks about Montreal. We talk of home like exiles do, but I'm going back any day and he's not. Not yet. Not for a long time.

He tells me his family are farmers near St. Jean-Port Jolie. A cousin raises pigs, another has a dairy farm. That's where Marcel learned his trade. "Trent-six métiers, trent-six misères," he says. "Do you have this expression in English?"

The expression's new.

The misère is palpable.

He talked to his kids not long ago. The conversation with the boy, André, was cold. "I think he blames me for what happened," Marcel says. "But my daughter, she wants to come and live with me."

He stares at his cup. His eyes are wet.

Michelle the waitress stubs out her cigarette. The guy at the other end of the counter reads the weekly *Inuvik Drum*. Nobody looks like they're paying attention. Everyone's all ears.

"She cleaned me out. There was two thousand dollars in the bank for their education. The money's all gone. She spent it on him." Him is the young Romanian.

"I don't know what he gets from this. Maybe he gets his citizenship. Me, I miss my kids. I raised my kids. I taught them to walk."

Michelle pours refills of sour coffee. She projects an air of sympathy as strong as any perfume. Marcel tears open a package of powdered artificial cream. "My wife says she likes her life now. I think she's a good actor."

What's he going to do? Eventually he'll get holidays. After he puts in a year on the job. After a year in Inuvik. He wants to see his kids in Montreal.

He'll wait as long as he has to.

GOOD SAMARITAN

We were in our hundreds in the métro. We might have been a single giant beast. Our eyes were glazed, and we moved slowly, like a river in the winter under the weight of ice. Our arms were heavy with packages. 'Twas the season.

He lay on the floor.

We stopped flowing then. We snagged on him. I was on my way into the métro. I had a book for my nephew and a couple of jars of mincemeat. I had plum pudding, and I had music and books for her. I stopped at the head of the stairs and looked.

He didn't move.

He lay sprawled in his heavy, unzipped parka. His big white belly spilled over his baggy pants. His eyes were closed. He lay on his back. I couldn't tell if he was breathing.

Two old women in fur coats stopped and shook their fur-hatted heads, as if to say, "Tsk-tsk, it's a shame." Then they took hold of the railing and each other, and they walked downstairs together, one step at a time.

Kids in knots of three and four also stopped to take a look. Some wore baggy clothes and stocking caps, some wore windbreakers and sneakers, some chewed gum. The kids came close, but no closer. They peered at the fallen man. They'd seen stuff like this on TV. They bent to look, the way they'd bend to drink from the fountain at school. So as not to get splashed.

The crowd was swelling now, and some of the shoppers pushed by with a quick look of annoyance. Progress was getting difficult. People looked at the man and they looked at each other and they spoke in shared whispers.

The man lay still. He lay on his back. One of his legs was crossed over the other. His arms were at his sides, palms up. You could tell what people were thinking—this man looks like fresh death.

Suddenly a young girl approached. She stepped forward and reached out her hand and held it over the man's mouth, tentatively, as if he might bite. Then just as suddenly she drew away and stepped back. Was he breathing? Couldn't tell.

Someone bumped into me. The man on the floor was holding up traffic, and so was I. Somebody ought to do something, I thought. And then a woman in a blue trenchcoat took charge.

She put her briefcase down. She put two fingers against the side of the man's neck. A guy with a pony tail, emboldened by the sight of her, moved forward to help. The woman said something, and then they rolled the man onto his side.

It wasn't easy. They pulled at him, they poked at him. No response. I joined the ranks of people with their mouths open. We looked helpless and stupid. We looked as if we were on TV.

Security now made a perimeter around the two Samaritans. Security was in plainclothes and looked like kids—the boy was tall and blond, with a buzz-cut and work boots; the girl was stocky, in a duffel coat and jeans. Together, they pushed the gawkers back. Let's give him some air, they said.

The ponytail walked over to the métro ticket booth and the ticket-taker picked up his phone. Ponytail returned for one last word with the woman in the trenchcoat, and then he went on his way. The girl security guard had a phone on her hip. She, too, made a call.

Now an old man pushed his way through the crowd. He had a few things on his mind. He asked the boy security guard what was wrong with the fallen man. The security guard said, "He's sick. Stand back, give him some air."

The old man said, "I'm sick myself. He's sick in the head." He sounded angry. He pointed a finger at the fallen man. "I'm sick myself. He's not sick. I'm sick." The security guard didn't argue. He moved the old man along.

Now a couple of métro police were kneeling by the fallen man, and the good Samaritan in the blue trenchcoat stood up. Her job was done. She picked up her briefcase and walked away.

I followed her.

Excuse me, you're very courageous, what's your name? "Sylvie." Are you a nurse? "No." How did you know what to do? "I took a St. John's ambulance course a few months ago." Is he going to be okay? "Well, he was breathing."

Why did you stop to help him? "He was lying on his back. It wasn't natural." What was the reason for rolling him over? "So he wouldn't choke if he spit up."

What's wrong with him? "I think he's just drunk." You're very brave. "Oh, no," she said. What do you do for a living? "I'm an accountant." Were you on your way to a meeting? "Yes, but I was going to do a bit of shopping first; now I won't get my shopping done, I'll just go to my meeting."

It takes courage, to stop like that. "No, I'm just glad I could help." And then she joined the crowd and disappeared.

Now the métro cops were lifting the man to his feet. He was rubbery. They held him by the elbows, and the crowd went on its way. Drunk is less interesting than dead.

The drunk man was confused. He tried to put on his toque. His fingers were working in slow motion. The cops led him away, holding him tenderly as he swayed. I followed them up an escalator.

Outside, the snow was falling lightly. There was an ambulance waiting on the street. The ambulance men were hauling out a stretcher. "Put that away," said the cops. "He's drunk." The ambulance drove off.

"Put on your gloves," said the cops to the man. "Get some air," said the cops. "Take a deep breath. Are you all right?" The drunk squinted at the falling snow.

An affirmative kind of squint.

BAFFIN HOUSE

The Inuit are masters of the harshest environment in the world. They are not startled by anything they see. But there is nothing in the Arctic to prepare them for the sight, the sound, the smell of Montreal.

This what they say when they come here: The noise of the city makes me tired. It is too hot. There are too many cars. Everything moves too fast. The buildings are so tall you cannot imagine it, even if you have seen them on TV.

The Inuit come here when they are sick, when there is no help for them in the tiny nursing stations of the North. They come when their cancers are ready to burst, and the hospital in Iqaluit can do no more for them.

They stay in a quiet stone residence called Baffin House, on a leafy street in Côte des Neiges. There are more trees in front of this house than there are on the whole of Baffin Island. There are no trees on Baffin Island.

Neither you nor I could survive in the North alone. The land would swallow us up. It is the same when the *kamik* is on the other foot. The Inuit need a city guide when they come to Montreal.

Meet Pitseola Ineak. It is her job to greet the Inuit who come here for medical help. She visits patients. She escorts people to the hospital. She interprets for the doctors. This is what the patients say to her:

My head aches. *Niakunguyunga.* I have pain here. *Uvuna aniayunga.* I feel very weak. *Nukikitnaluyunga.* I do not like this. *Una piuginginaku.*

The language is a thick soup of syllables, and translation isn't always easy. There are no words in Inuktitut for CAT scan.

It is hard in other ways. A patient from the North may choose to go home after being diagnosed with a fatal but treatable disease.

Pitseola must try to persuade them to take treatment. Some people choose to die at home.

Today, Pitseola has two patients: a man is going to the General for the results of an electrocardiogram, and a young mother must bring her daughter to the Children's Hospital for tests.

Pitseola meets Jacob at Baffin House. He is small and well-muscled, compactly formed. He is also silent and expectant. He is no stranger to the city. He tells the doctor he's been to the hospital in Montreal twice before. Once for a cut. And once when he punctured his lung in a car accident.

The doctor cuffs his arm, takes his blood pressure, listens to his heart with a stethoscope. "Any problems with the lungs recently, Jacob?" "I had pneumonia this spring," he says.

The doctor takes Jacob's right hand and checks his pulse. A thick and ragged scar runs crazily across the wrist. The doctor's eyes widen. "What happened here?" he asks. Jacob chooses not to answer. He's already answered. He was here once before, for a cut. And now it's healed.

The doctor tells Pitseola he must go and find some charts. When he returns, he says he has found an aneurysm in Jacob's aorta. The aneurysm is ready to burst. Jacob must be admitted at once. Pitseola repeats what the doctor says in Inuktitut. The doctor looks at her. She looks at Jacob. Jacob looks away. Silence.

Finally, he rolls down his sleeves and nods his head. He was not expecting to have to stay. His face is without expression, but you can tell he is thinking hard. He is thinking of his family at home. From an open window, a jackhammer chips away at the sidewalk. Its beat is erratic, and louder than anybody's heart.

Pitseola and Jacob sit together outside Admitting. He looks perfectly healthy, but his aorta is a ticking bomb. They talk softly, as if they were listening. Tick, tick, tick.

The language they speak is suited perfectly to the floe edge, but exotic on the edge of a hospital bench. When people hear them talking, they are startled, and they stare. The sound is unlike anything anyone here has ever heard.

When it is nearly noon, a man pushes a sandwich cart down the hall. He sings "Hot-Coffee Sandwiches. Muff-fins. Dough-nuts. Ice-a-cold drinks." It is a song unlike anything heard in Pond Inlet.

Finally, there is a room. Pitseola escorts Jacob upstairs and leaves him alone by his bed. He is nervous, alert. There are more people in this hospital than there are back home in Pond. Pitseola says she will call on him later, and bring him what he needs from his suitcase back at Baffin House.

On her way out, she spots another Inuk sitting in a wheelchair. This man is a hunter. He knows how to read the land. His eyes are wide open, his ears hear every sound. He is sitting up straight. He reads the lobby of the hospital. Pitseola stops to say hello. *Qanuiipit.*

The man has recently had a stroke. His right arm is weak. He cannot raise it without effort. This is a great worry. Hunting is how he provides for his family. It is his only source of income. He got a narwhal this summer. He will need therapy on his arm before he is able to get another. He will not have that therapy here.

He has chosen to go home.

After lunch, Pitseola leads the young mother and her daughter through a maze of shortcuts in the Montreal Children's Hospital. In Inuktitut, the word for mother is *Anana*, and the word for daughter is *Panik*.

Anana is wearing an *amautiq*, a traditional parka with a hood in the back for the baby. She is wearing jeans and a T-shirt, and she is chewing gum. She does not speak any English. She knows there is a problem with Panik's heart. The doctors have found a tiny hole, and they want to do more tests.

The ultrasound technician is pink and pretty, with blonde hair and perfect make-up. She smears Panik's chest with goo and passes a device like a microphone over the baby's chest.

Panik lies on her back, her arms thrown wide apart. On a television monitor, her heart appears as a tiny liquid fist, clenching and unclenching in a plasmic sea. Anana blows a pink bubble with her gum. She and Pitseola watch the screen carefully. A doctor explains the problem: inside Panik's heart, red blood is leaking into the chamber for blue blood.

Pitseola translates. There is no expression on Anana's face. What mother can comprehend the sight of her baby's pierced and beating heart? Panik will need an operation next year. The operation is serious, but simple to perform. *Taima.*

In the back of a cab on the way home to Baffin House, Panik burbles merrily in the language of babies. Pitseola and Anana laugh and talk together. You cannot understand what they are saying.

There is no need to translate.

SAILOR WAS A BLEEDER

Ladies and gentlemen, boys and girls.

Actually, there are very few ladies and gentlemen in the audience today. A fierce storm has pillowed the streets with snow, and most of the available adults are at home digging out their cars. What we have instead is a generous scattering of rude and raucous neighbourhood kids, and people who don't drive.

Welcome to an afternoon of World All-Star Wrestling in the Grover Auditorium of the Snowdon YMHA. Your ring announcer today is Dave Singer, and your timekeeper is the legendary Omer Marchesseault.

Omer Marchesseault, the man who refereed the most famous wrestling match in Montreal history, André the Giant vs. Don Leo Jonathan. May 29, 1972. It was a dirty fight. Marchesseault disqualified the Giant and then, as if to prove a point, he disqualified him again. In the ensuing mêlée, someone ripped the hairpiece off Dave Singer's head. There is no chance of that today.

Singer's going topless.

There are five matches on today's card. The matches have been organized by Andy Ellison as a fundraiser for the Snowdon YMHA. Andy, a Snowdon alumnus, is a wrestler and a sociology student at Concordia.

He is a big guy for a sociologist.

We are killing time backstage when Ironman Peter McLeod passes by. "As-tu l'assurance?" he asks. Ironman's cut his pinky. It is a huge pinky. It is a teeny cut. Andy tells Ironman what he can do with his insurance and his little finger. The thought of it makes them laugh.

The rest of the wrestlers are getting ready in the dressing room upstairs. Dynamite Dan tapes his wrists, and out of consideration for his opponent, he smears his armpits with deodorant. I see his arms and shoulders bulge. He is one of those big men who happens to be small.

When he isn't wrestling, Dynamite Dan's a plasterer. Before he started to wrestle and before he started to plaster, he was a boxer in Florida. Bareknuckle fights, illegal fights. Dynamite's nose has never been broken, but he tells me he has floating ribs.

"They're floating now," he says.

Wildside Phil Slayer adjusts his trunks. Phil's been in the business for five or six years. He started wrestling in Newfoundland with the Sailor White retirement tour. "Sailor was a bleeder," says Wildside Phil. "Every night, he would bleed and bleed and bleed." It's a good thing the Sailor retired.

Nobody has that much blood.

Wildside Phil is another of these heavyweight sociologists, which makes me wonder if the sociology they teach at Concordia is no holds barred.

The audience is getting restless. They want blood. They'll get it in dribs and drabs. Patient P-13, a huge man with a shaved head who has been pacing back and forth in a hospital gown, steps barefoot on a piece of broken glass. He'll fight in spite of it.

Sailor White would love him.

In the first match of the afternoon, Jason the Terrible takes on Dynamite Dan. Jason wears a hockey mask and a pair of mechanic's overalls. He holds a canoe paddle in his hands. Dynamite Dan's floating ribs are in trouble.

This is a good vs. evil match.

I watch carefully as Jason slams his opponent. Dynamite Dan explodes as he hits the mat. Then Jason throws him through the ropes and on top of some ringside chairs. Dan falls off the chairs and onto the floor of the auditorium. Ouch.

There is a small cut on the back of Dan's thigh. Here's your blood, kids. There isn't much, but it's real. Dan bounces back into the ring. Jason picks him up and flops on him. In the fight between good and evil, good goes down for the count. Jason glares at the jeering crowd.

Backstage, Dan is breathing hard. The inside of his lip is split, and the back of his right thigh trickles red. All in a day's work.

In the next match, Cowboy Grant Grey takes on Michel

Frenette for the light heavyweight championship of the world. "It's a big world," says the laconic Omer Marchesseault.

Frenette and Grant Grey are no more light heavyweights than I am, but it doesn't seem to matter. Dave Singer tells the crowd that the championship belt contains four genuine rubies. So did the pin I bought my mom when I was ten.

Grant Grey is a little gadfly. He insults the kids, the kids insult him. He and Frenette take turns throwing each other in the air and slamming each other to the mat. Frenette bites Grey's hand. In retaliation, Grey thumps Frenette into a highly thespian coma, kicks him in the ribs, chokes him for good measure, then sits on his head for a three-count.

Omer Marchesseault rings the bell.

It is a red fire alarm bell. Marchesseault hits it vigorously with a socket wrench. The new world champion holds up his belt. Then he smashes it down on the dazed noggin of the fallen champ. Heavy hangs the head that wore the crown.

The crowd goes wild.

I am trying to see if the matches are rigged. I find no direct evidence. There have been whispered conversations to which I was not privy, but there is also a great deal of spontaneity between the ropes. That's all these kids are asking for. Spontaneity, and a little blood.

Match three features Patient P-13 vs. Bad Boy Bouchard. The Patient limps gingerly on his punctured foot. He is winning the match until he is disqualified for massaging Bad Boy's head with brass knuckles. The match is mercifully short, perhaps in deference to the Patient's foot.

Backstage, Michel Frenette, the newly former light heavyweight champion of the world—this world, anyway—takes a deep drag from a smoke and a long drink from a can of coke. He's bouncing on the balls of his feet. He's ready to go again.

After Wildside Phil Slayer clobbers the hapless Rock 'n Roll Man, it's time for the last match of the day. The heavyweight championship of the world. Ironman vs. Andy Ellison of Côte St. Luc.

Andy is the hometown favourite, a hero to the kids. Ironman smashes him into the turnbuckle, and the hometown favourite buckles to his knees. "I'm the best there is. I'm the best in the world," observes Ironman with contempt.

Omer Marchesseault and Dave Singer watch carefully. In low voices, they speak the tough-guy poetry of wrestling. Figure-four leg lock. Step-over toe-hold. Short-arm scissors. The poetry of the people.

Some kid yells, "Ironman, your belly's bigger than your butt," and suddenly the tide of the match turns. Ironman is pinned for a count of three and Andy Ellison of Côte St. Luc is crowned the heavyweight champeen.

Kids surround him in the ring and slap him on the back.

The other wrestlers have packed their gym bags, collected their expenses and gone home in the snow. Ellison stays behind and poses for instamatic photographs. Ironman sits alone, exhausted, on a stool in the dressing room.

"We do this for charity," he says. "We do it for Andy. Andy is a good guy." Ironman opens the envelope containing his expense money. He looks inside.

He counts two five dollar bills.

THE HAYSTACK IN SEARCH OF THE NEEDLE

To put a ring in Bruna's navel is to paint the lily.

But it's Bruna's navel and she's old enough to know what she's doing, and anyway you can't tell kids these days a thing. She chooses a steel ring with a red agate bead.

Pierre lays out his tools. One pair of red-handled pliers. One ring spreader, high-quality, purchased at Canadian Tire. A pair of forceps with a circular tip. Disinfectants. And a fourteen gauge needle, thick as a pencil lead and sharp enough to pierce flesh easily.

He marks a spot above Bruna's navel with a red pen. Perfect. He clamps the top lip of her navel with the forceps. Perfect. Bruna's brought a friend for moral support, and Pierre asks him to hold the forceps straight, and to pull them forward slightly. This is an intimate experience. Bruna breathes deeply.

Her navel is perfect, an innie.

And I watch as Pierre pushes the needle through the red spot on the flap of skin between the forceps. Bruna breathes again, sharply. and says, "Oh, wow!" Pierre inserts the ring and attaches the agate bead.

She says, "I feel it in my skin. It's like an object, really weird." I take her word for it. There seems to be no pain. There is no blood. The boyfriend's glad it's over.

Pierre operates out of a white room with black trim. There is black-and-white linoleum on the floor. There are cabinets filled with nose and navel and nipple rings. The room is in his apartment, over a fruit store in the Plateau.

He does this for a living, but for him it's more than that. It is art, administered through flesh. It is also a way, he says, for people to take control of their bodies.

I think it's tribalism, but I'm here to learn.

Brenda's eighteen. She has a close-cropped Tinkerbell haircut, she's come in with her girlfriend and she wants a stud in her tongue.

I can't imagine why. I've bitten my tongue. I know what that's like. The pain had me rolling on the floor. I ask her why she wants it done. She gives me a look. Stupid question. She doesn't answer right away.

She says she's tired, she's having trouble concentrating. Brenda and her friend tell me they work in the field of music promotion. Later they revise their resumé and say they work the coat check at a club. Whatever.

Brenda finally says, "I find it sexy. I'm just experimenting with different, um, thingies."

Brenda's friend is an impossibly beautiful girl with perfect features and the kind of bee-stung mouth that is boring in fashion photos but is breathtaking in real life. I begin to feel like a haystack in search of a needle.

Brenda's friend wears a ring in her lower lip. On her it is adornment, not disfigurement. She also has a ring in her nostril and several piercings in her ears. I realize I'm staring.

Which proves that attractive people can wear whatever they want and do whatever they want to themselves and still look good.

Brenda's tongue is perfectly pink, the colour of bubble gum, and it curls at the tip. Pierre cleans it and dries it off. Brenda says, "Ah" as if she were at the doctor's. Pierre makes a little mark in the centre of the tongue, an inch or so back from the tip.

He clamps her tongue with the forceps. Again, he asks her friend to hold them. The friend pulls, Brenda's eyes widen, Pierre tells her to take three deep breaths. On three he pushes the needle through her tongue.

Brenda says, "Ah. Ah. Ah." The needle remains embedded in her pink flesh while Pierre reaches for the stud. There is no blood. She says, "Uh. Ah. Ah." And quick as a flash, Pierre removes the needle and inserts the stud and screws in the ball that will keep it in place. I ask Brenda if there's any pain. She says, "Adrenalin is going all over me. This is cool. It's so cool."

I ask Brenda's friend if she's ever snagged any of her rings on anything. She laughs. She says, "I caught my nose ring on the pillow this morning."

Afterwards, Pierre shows me his portfolio of photographs. He has glossy pictures of people who are stuck with jewellery in the usual places and some of people who have things stuck in places you can hardly imagine.

He is an intelligent young man, careful in his work and more thoughtful about what he is doing than any of the people who've come to see him so far.

I try not to gape at the photos. I see pictures of men who are pierced where I've caught myself in my zipper. He says he's pierced there, but I want proof. I'm about to ask Pierre to show me something I have never asked another man to show me. Then I see his picture in the portfolio, and I don't have to ask.

Piercing, he says, is not simply about adornment or pain. Some piercings can alter or even heighten sexual response. Some are gestures of defiance in the face of a world concerned solely with appearance. And some are just for fun. I'm not completely convinced, but I'm less skeptical than I was in the beginning.

Amber wants her tongue done, too.

She's eighteen with fair skin and straight red hair. She's wearing a T-shirt with a picture of a canary sleeping on a cloud. The canary is wearing a nightcap. Amber is wearing heavy black boots.

Why is she getting her tongue pierced? Because she works as a waitress and she can't have a ring in her lip, her nostril or her eyebrow at the restaurant where she works. Therefore, a stud in her tongue.

Amber's brought a friend—everybody seems to bring a friend—whose nose and ears and tongue are pierced. How old she was when her ears were done? "Three," says the friend. "My mother told me if I got my ears pierced, I could have a hamster."

She's also pierced where her baby's going to nurse if she ever decides to give birth. I don't know what her mother thinks of that. The thought of it makes me shiver.

Amber asks Pierre if it's going to hurt. Without waiting for the answer, she tells him she bought apple sauce today, and then she laughs. Pierre tells her it isn't going to hurt. It doesn't hurt.

An hour later, Lorna comes in alone. She is an anthropology student at Concordia. She wants her navel done. Because she's by herself, Pierre asks me to help.

As a Piercer's Assistant Trainee, it is my job to hold the forceps straight and pull the top lip of her bellybutton forward. Lorna's nervous. I am, too.

Pierre waits until we take our three deep breaths. I hold the forceps and stare at her little innie. On the third breath, the needle goes through just like that. Lorna draws in her breath. Once again, there seems to be no pain.

Finally, the last customer of the day.

She is a china doll of a girl named Evelyn. She has tiny perfect features. She says she wants to change her look. After some discussion about the placement of a ring in her nostril, she closes her eyes and takes deep breaths. And then she's pierced. A tiny bead of blood gathers around the needle.

It is brighter than the bead she's chosen for the ring.

GOD HELPS THE CHILD IN WEST END MONTREAL

Rain taps at the windows of third-floor apartments, rain splashes the trunks of scrawny trees, rain eats the last gritty mounds of snow in Little Burgundy. A cold rain falls everywhere in the west end, except on the statue of Oscar Peterson.

That's because there is no statue of Oscar Peterson.

Sitting in a swivel chair in a neighbourhood barber shop, looking out the window at the falling rain, Bob White wonders why this city won't honour the greatest jazz piano player in the world.

"The President of the United States comes up here, he doesn't know anything about Canada, but he knows Oscar Peterson's from Montreal."

Half a dozen black heads nod in unison.

Bob's got a point. He's got a lot of points. He bounces from one to another in a day-long, free-form rap about race and responsibility, ranging over the whole city, but starting where he always starts. In the west end.

"Don't call it Little Burgundy. There is no Little Burgundy. That's just code for 'black.' This is the west end. Come on, I want to show you something." He slips a hipster's cap over his slick head and reaches for his trenchcoat.

Half a block away, on the corner of a street where the poverty is so real you can smell it in the air, he points to an ordinary little dépanneur.

Ordinary but for one thing. On the front wall of the store, in crude blue letters, someone has spray-painted the words "Speak French" and "Englishit."

Seen close up, it's sickening.

Who are the punks with the paint? Bob White knows, and so does the woman who runs the store, but she doesn't want to talk. All she'll say is this: "Where there is chaos, there are people who will take advantage."

Bob White says, "You think this is bad? I'll show you something else." Something else, in the same blue paint, is the eloquently racist "101" sprayed on an English-language plaque on the wall of the historic Union United Church.

Is it about race? Is it about language? Is the unease in the west end really about who's a Montrealer and who isn't? It doesn't really matter.

Except it does.

It's always mattered if your skin is black.

Because of the neglect, the poverty and the withering social tension, the people of this neighbourhood do what they can to look after themselves: The West End Sports Association runs a tab for the needy at a local butcher shop. A shoe store across the street specializes in cheap shoes. God helps the child, as it were.

It's not enough.

Bob White wants to restore black pride. The statue of Peterson is one way. There are others. He thinks the people who run the jazz festival should put bands on flatbed trucks, bringing music—and tourist money—into the neighbourhood which gave Oscar to the world.

He wants the city to build a gym for west end kids. He points to an empty park where there ought to be an outdoor rink. Sports is a way up for some, and a way out for others. The football player Tommy Kane grew up in this neighbourhood. So did the basketball player Trevor Williams.

It's not a question of handouts, it's a question of getting back a little of what you give—blacks pay taxes, too.

Now Bob's on a roll across the city, walking a mile a minute and talking twice as fast. There's no stopping the flow of ideas. He points to a vacant lot across from the Faubourg and says it ought to be filled with outdoor chess tables.

He says there ought to be a series of plaques on lamp-posts leading down the street from the old Forum to the new one, one in honour of each of Montreal's Stanley Cups. A kind of outdoor Hockey Walk of Fame.

"The people who run this city aren't tapped into the past. Or the present. Therefore, there is no future." He's got a point, he's got a dozen points, every one of them is reinforced by a pothole, a vacant lot, an empty building.

Bob lets up only when he stops for lunch at Pick's, a little Jamaican success story across from the Vendôme métro. For the past six years, Pick has been frying fish and making pots of goat's-head soup in a basement apartment in NDG. Selling black market suppers under the nose of his landlord. With the tacit support of his hungry neighbours.

Pick went legit in January.

Bob polishes off a plate of snapper with red beans and rice, downs a glass of soursop juice, then heads next door to look in on the journalist Egbert Gaye. Egbert couldn't find a job four years ago when he graduated from Concordia, so he started his own paper, the monthly *Community Contact*.

The message is clear.

If you're black in this town, you'd better look after yourself. Bob White keeps pushing, one kid at a time, one community at a time, one question at a time:

Why is there no plaque in memory of Dr. Charles Drew, the black McGill grad who invented blood plasma? Why is there nothing to commemorate Charles Latimer, the black man who brought electric lights to Montreal? Most of all, why is there there no statue in honour of the great jazz pianist?

The questions keep coming.

The rain keeps falling.

Everywhere, except on Oscar.

WALTER AUBIE

"Have you had any acting experience?" asks the director. He is addressing two young women standing on a stage in a chilly, tatty theatre in the belly of a landmark downtown church. "We did some improvisation at school," they say.

"Fine, let's see you improvise—you are in a waiting room, you are getting impatient, one of you starts talking." Walter Aubie, intent, listens closely.

He is a slight, handsome man with lively eyes and a sense of *gravitas,* no mean feat considering that he is dressed in an oversized red sweater, green work pants, fuschia legwarmers, and pink socks.

The two young women don't know it, but they are part of a dramatic comeback—two years ago, Walter Aubie was hit by a car while crossing the street. How badly was he hurt ? He draws a line from his ankle to his forehead, and says, "I was broken from here to here. Would you like a look?"

He rolls up his sleeve. There are several long, thick scars running up his forearm, the after-effects of reconstructive surgery. "Feel this," he says, pointing to his elbow. I feel several hard, round lumps. "There are 21 pieces of metal in my arm."

Now he's working his way back into shape. He's auditioning amateurs for a production of *The Odd Couple.* You've seen the TV series, if not the film. It's his way of giving thanks for his recovery. Any money he manages to raise will be donated to the homeless.

Aubie's stage experience goes back thirty years in Montreal. He went to theatre school with Richard Monette, who now directs the Stratford Festival, and he acted with Chomedy's Hana Gartner in the old days.

He started teaching at the Montreal Children's Theatre School in 1960. Since then, he says, "I have taught ten thousand children, and I have played every prince, king and monster imaginable."

While he puts the two young women through their paces, an older man comes in, squinting—he's looking for the audition, and his glasses are fogged from the cold. He's wearing a parka and a cap with ear flaps. He's bearded. He blows his nose. His name is Ray.

Aubie offers him a script and a chance to read as either the fastidious Felix or the messy Oscar. Ray says, "I'll be Oscar. I'm a drinking man, myself."

Ray/Oscar takes the stage with the two young women, and there is something instantly watchable about the man; he delivers his lines like a broadcaster describing a home run.

In the play, the girls are masseuses who live in the flat upstairs from the Odd Couple. On stage, it is supposed to be summer; the girls tell Oscar they have been sitting in front of their open fridge, in nature's own. It is not easy to deliver this line. It is chilly in the church, and it is thirty below outside.

Walter thanks them crisply, and invites them to a callback audition next week. He says, with theatrical emphasis, "I want you to know there is no money involved in this play. Whatso. Ever. There is no pay. And there will be no charge at the door. We will ask for a donation."

He has already asked for volunteers—it turns out Ray is Walter's cousin, corralled at a family gathering a couple of weeks ago.

But this is an open audition, and there are surprises. Halfway through the afternoon, a man named Mark enters the theatre, at once tentative and confident. He attends St. James United, and he's got the acting bug.

Walter invites him on stage and the two men act together, walking around the stage in an improvised choreography. Mark is no stranger to acting—he teaches literacy, he's used to holding people's attention. He and Walter clip each others' lines so the dialogue sounds close to conversation.

Walter's having fun.

And then Jules walks in, and the fun gets grander—Jules is a big guy, with a barrel chest, thick arms, thick glasses, a thatch of hair and a voice as deep as a well. Jules has done some evangelical acting—he has been a Pontius Pilate, a shepherd and an angel. He is big enough to have been an archangel.

Jules has Oscar the messy sportswriter written all over him. With a French accent, that is. And when Jules and Mark act together, the dialogue rattles like a replay of the referendum.

Felix: *You said I irritated you.*

Oscar: *You said you irritated me, I didn't say it.*

Felix: *Then what did you say?*

Oscar: *I don't know what I said.*

Canada and Quebec.

By the end of the day, Walter has auditioned five men and the two young women. He could mount the play with the actors he has, if he had to. The only problem, he says, is Samuel French—which is to say, the rights; Neil Simon's plays aren't cheap, even for amateurs.

Aubie has written to the author, asking for a freebie. It has to be a freebie. There is no money. Money could be an obstacle. But Walter Aubie has been tossed by a car and bounced back, and a little thing like rights isn't going to throw him now.

The Odd Couple is scheduled to open this spring.

KIDS, COURTING

She has dirty blond hair. She's sitting on the last seat of the subway car. Her legs are crossed; one foot dangles with the rhythm of the train. There are two boys sitting on the dirty floor beside her.

She tells them she's 15 years old. She's doing all the talking, but the boys are the ones on the make. They've got grins on their faces. They hang on her every word.

She says "I used to steal hair dye." She says this easily, as if it were part of a story that begins "Once upon a time, long ago and far away..."

It's rush hour. She's talking louder than she has to. she doesn't care who hears what she says. The subway car is full of old people going home from work. She doesn't care who hears.

She's wearing a baggy shirt and an army jacket. She's carrying a backpack. There are crude ink drawings on her jeans, and there's a four-letter word scrawled on the backpack with a ball-point pen. The word starts with F, but it's only got three letters. It's a small backpack.

The train pulls away from the station. The people around her are tired, numb from the day. They're hanging on the handrails, packed together, swaying gently.

The girl has a gold ring in her nostril, gold studs in her ears. Her hands are dirty and dainty, and her nails are closely bitten. She says "I used to steal hair dye, blond and purple, from the Jean Coutu in Rosemont."

The boys nod their heads at this, as if they never pay for anything themselves. The girl says, "I never paid for hair dye in my life until I got caught."

The train is racing through the tunnel. You can tell how long it's been since she got caught. Her hair is dirty and her roots are one inch long.

She says, "Now if I steal and get caught, I go to Shawbridge." The two boys are wearing baggy clothes and hooded sweats. They seem to think that's cool—you know, girls are cool, stealing's cooler, girls who steal are coolest.

The boys grin broadly. As if Shawbridge is no big deal. From the looks on their faces, you'd think it was stupid not to steal. Because the stuff is just there on the shelf. Because what difference does it make? Because only people with jobs pay cash.

There is a pause in the conversation until the girl observes, "I have a way with cops. When I got caught, I was so good with them." As if she were in charge. She probably was. She train is rocking from side to side.

She says, "I was so good with them. They were giving me coffee and doughnuts. I was like 'Oh, I feel so bad.'" A mock-sad look on her face. The boys are really grinning now. If it's cool to steal, it's way cool to fool cops.

The boy with the red hood takes the girl's left hand in both of his. She pretends not to notice. As if it's not her hand he's holding. As if it's someone else's hand.

The train pulls into a station. People get off, people get on. They crowd around the kids, but not too close. You never know what kids might do. The boy is examining her palm.

The girl says, "If I smoke in my room and get caught, I get thrown out of the house. But I don't care. I do it all the time. There's nothing to it. I use Secret Antiperspirant spray to mask the smell. I spray it around the room."

You can't hide the smell of smoke. You give her points for trying. You take points away for not trying hard enough.

The red-hooded boy holds her hand in his. He traces her life line, her heart line, her head line with his finger. She's trying not to pay attention. He tells her, "This line is your mansion. This line is your swimming pool. This line is your tennis court." The other boy guffaws.

The girl is smiling, chewing gum. She might end up in court, but for the moment she's being courted. Red-hood traces the tip of his finger lightly over the palm of her hand. Her palm is tingling. She knows it's her hand now.

The train pulls into my station. I want to stay and listen to everything the girl has to say to the boys. But I get off and go home instead. I'm hungry and I'm tired and I'm angry. I'm angry at the girl. I don't want her to steal. I'm angry at the boys. I want them to leave her alone. I'm angry thinking of her pregnant or in jail.

I can't stop thinking of her dirty hair.

A DAY AT DECISION HOUSE

A dozen men and a woman are sitting in a loose circle of cheap chairs in a dingy room in what used to be a school in Pointe St. Charles. The men live in the school. They're junkies and they're thieves, they're boozers, users and abusers.

The woman is a therapist. Her name is Linda. The school used to be called Canon O'Meara. Now it's called Decision House. Welcome to rehab.

It isn't easy to get here.

You have to screw up good. Swinging a knife on a dozen cops is one way. Armed robbery is another. Using drugs is the easiest way of all. Whichever way you choose, you get here through the courts.

Sometimes, if you buy into the program, you can go home from here. Other times—say, if you're staring at a big bit from the courts—you get out of rehab and you go straight to jail. Nobody likes to go to jail. Jail's full of drugs, and guys who haven't dropped their image.

These men have been up since six, sweeping floors, doing chores, eating toast. If the school were a fancy hotel and the men were wearing suits instead of jeans, you'd think they were brokers or salesmen roughing it together at a team-building session. But they're not salesmen. They're thieves and knife artists, second. They're addicts and alkies, first.

Linda starts the meeting. She tells Rob to take off his cap. She asks him how his weekend went. You don't bullshit Linda. Which is to say, if you did, you'd be bullshitting yourself. Rob is just a kid. The men look out the window. The sun is shining, the sky is blue. It's eight a.m. It's early for this kind of stuff. Or maybe it's too late.

Nah, it's never too late.

Rob grins and says the weekend went okay. He's wearing gym shorts and a T-shirt with a map of France. Linda asks him if he's got much more time to do. Rob says two more months. Linda asks, "Are you sure?" Rob says it depends on his lawyer.

Linda pins him fast. She says, "It depends on you, Rob. It doesn't depend on your lawyer. It depends on you."

George rolls his eyes upward and grins. He's heard it all before. He knows the program. He's a little scrapper with water-slicked hair who looks like he just stepped out of a gym in a black-and-white movie from the 40's. George coughs and lights up a smoke. Linda works the talk around the room.

Every man gets a turn in the hot seat. It's part of the program, it's the way these guys keep each other straight. They're down to their last chance. All they've got is each other. They may be good cons, but they can't con themselves in this room.

Beaver slouches in when it's Barry's turn.

Beaver's dressed for a morning court date in a sharp blue suit. He looks pissed off. He says he wants out of the program. He wants a job that doesn't bore him, a decent place to live. He wants a girl. He says maybe today he'll tell the judge he's going to take his time.

There is a psychic sucking of air.

What Beaver means is he's thinking of skipping out of rehab and finishing his sentence in jail. It's the quickest way to get out, but every man in the room knows you can't stay straight in jail. You can get anything you want in jail. Beaver's been straight for a long time now. The other guys like Beaver, and they're worried about what will happen if he takes his time.

Somebody out front calls "Let's go." Beaver touches his tie, sticks his hands in his pockets and slouches out of the room. He's got a decision to make.

The talk continues around the room. Mike gets up from his chair. He's a tall man in a fog, partly because he's taking medication for paranoia. His doctor gives him a needle once a month, with pills for the side effects. He goes to the bathroom and pukes. Then he tells Linda he wants to talk to his lawyer. Mike always wants his lawyer.

Linda says maybe later.

"Brent, how was your weekend?"

Brent leans his shoulder against the desk. His shoulder is a stump. He lost his arm in a boating accident when he was in his teens. He poured the insurance settlement up his nose and down his throat. How much was the settlement?

A quarter-mil, U.S.

"I've fuckin' had it with the program," he says.

Brent's still smarting from an incident a couple of weeks ago. Somebody called him names. Brent thinks he should have popped the guy. Nobody's got a right to say to another guy what that guy said to Brent. He's still tied up in knots.

Brent's temper is an issue.

The group leans on him. Let it go, Brent. Don't let that guy live in your head. Addicts can't afford resentment. Work the program. Use the tools. Brent loses his cool and leaves the room.

It's time for lunch. Mike asks Linda if he can call his lawyer. Linda says he's in court. Mike says his lawyer always calls right back. Brent is fuming somewhere in the building; you can feel the glower, even if you can't see it. Everyone's worried that Beaver's going to take his time.

Kenny hands me a plate of cold cuts and potato salad. Kenny's a likable guy. His father kicked him out of the house when he was nine years old. He has a ready smile and a history of trouble with knives.

The food is left over from the AA ball game on the weekend. It looks okay for rehab food, but the plate is heaped too high. I demur, but Kenny says if you're going to hang with the boys, you eat what the boys eat.

I take the plate.

It's been a long day and it's only half past eleven.

Dave says he had a rough weekend—on Saturday, a date he'd set up with his wife fell through. But then on Sunday they rented a movie and watched it holding hands. They've been married 22 years. He doesn't want to lose her.

Dave's a trucker; that is, he's a trucker when he has his license. Booze and pills got him so screwed up he'd dial 911 for directory assistance. And then the cops would come. And then he'd get, um, aggressive. Now he's in rehab, trying to get his shit together and looking at a charge of uttering death threats.

Paul takes all this in and smiles as he wipes tables. Paul's 29 years old. He's an Inuk from Sanikiluak. He swiped a bottle of rum from some construction workers when he was nine, and he's been drinking and doing drugs ever since. He came to Montreal last winter. He's been in rehab two weeks. He says his stomach hurts, but he can't afford to fill his prescription. Dave says, "You can still afford to smoke."

Bingo.

Paul's smile is a little sheepish. Dave's working the program. He wants Paul to work it, too. Some of the guys doing time in rehab went to school in this building when they were kids. Now they've come full circle.

A hell of a circle.

Barry shows me around—bedrooms upstairs, weight room downstairs. Kitchen and dining room, meeting room and offices on the middle floor. There is one shower for sixteen guys. The place is sort of clean and sort of depressing. Some of the windows are sort of broken, and covered over with plastic sheeting.

At first, I take Barry for a professional man—he's articulate and thoughtful, with a good haircut and clear blue eyes. He carries himself well, he's in good shape, he's good in group, and he works hard to help the other guys.

He's a professional, all right. His profession was robbing banks. Barry's thirty-five years old. He's spent fifteen years in jail. He's working on dropping his image. You want to like him. For his sake, you want the program to work.

The program is a mix of AA therapy and no-bullshit zen—you let it all hang out. You tell no lies to the group and the group will keep you straight until you can keep yourself straight. All the answers come from inside. You have to want to ask yourself the questions. That's what group is for.

And even though the meeting room has had a chance to air out from the morning session, the air is still sour with smoke. Everybody here uses tobacco except Derek, the bodybuilder, a clenched fist of a man whose biceps are bigger than my thighs.

Derek doesn't smoke, but he does a pack a day just breathing in this room. He was at the AA ball game on the weekend with some of the other guys from The House. How was it? "Let's not kid ourselves," he says. "I'm not normal. I had a good time. I made my presence felt."

I shudder to think how.

Now it's Johnny's turn.

How's Johnny today? Hard to say. Johnny never says much. A couple of words at a time. He's the only man in the room still on his twenty-four, which means he doesn't get out without supervision.

Johnny acts like he doesn't give a shit, but you can tell it pisses him off. He picks up from the morning theme—he picks up from Beaver and Brent—and says he wants out of the program. Barry jumps on his case.

"This is not a little problem, Johnny. You're a thief and an addict. They arrested you in your mother's home. You used a plastic gun. Get with the program, Johnny. Make it work for you."

George jumps in as soon as Barry's through, as if this were a tag-team act. George speaks with the authority of a man who's tried to kill himself and decided he wants to live. He's made that decision nine times: He shot bleach in his arm. He slashed at his jugular once and missed. He tried to hang himself twice but the rope broke both times. He's lucky to be in this room.

George knows bullshit when he sees it. He looks at Johnny and he looks around the room. He says, "Junk fucked up Johnny, it fucked up his brother, it fucked up a few friends of his. You wanna sell junk, Johnny? Where you gonna sell it? The gangs are taking over. There's no more room for a guy like you."

Johnny rolls his liquid eyes and looks up to the ceiling. There's a spider hanging from a thread. Johnny's smile is crooked. He doesn't want to stay, he doesn't want to go. He's looking at a big bit for armed robbery. The only guys he knows outside are users. The only guys he knows who are straight are in this room.

If I were him, I'd be scared.

The day ends with a game of volleyball in the yard outside. Group's hard. You have to work the tension off with something physical.

The men play a pretty loose game—a serve that bounces off the tree is good if it falls in. The ball goes back and forth. They keep it in bounds the way they keep each other in bounds, sometimes with a kick, sometimes with a slap, sometimes with a laugh.

Mike watches from the balcony. Brent smokes on the sidelines. Kenny wonders what happened to Beaver. Supper's almost ready. Beaver should have been home by now. Kenny says, "I think he took his time. I hope he didn't, but I think he took his time."

A hell of a decision, if he did.

MICKEY

Mickey leaned against a square of concrete in a tiny park near the student ghetto. I sat down beside him. You couldn't see us from the street. He pulled a bottle from the pocket of his baggy jeans and took his first drink of the day.

The smell of vodka sweetened the cold air. Mickey's in his forties, grizzled, dark-eyed and alert. He rolled a skinny smoke and lit it. The smoke curled up the side of his thick moustache. We were sitting in the shadows.

"If woting could change the sistem, it would be illigal," read the graffiti on the wall. You expect better spelling near the university, but Mickey agreed with the sentiment. Mickey's an itinerant. You need an address to wote.

He's slept in his share of doorways. A doorway is not an address. One winter he lived in the chalet on top of Mount Royal. That's no address, either. He'd sneak in as the place was being locked up for the night.

He says he spent two winters in a doghouse underneath the balcony of a home in Westmount. The doghouse was carpeted and insulated. The homeowners never knew he was there. Sometimes he'd watch them through a window.

He says he moved out of the doghouse when the government got him a room. He likes the room well enough. It's still a dog's life, as near as I can tell, but at least he gets a little welfare, and he doesn't have to panhandle.

He is more articulate than most of the men who roam the streets. He has half a degree in anthropology because he only went to classes half the time. Education's not the most important thing for a walking man.

"You see an itinerant with bad shoes, you know he doesn't care about himself." I look at Mickey's feet. He's wearing a decent pair of runners, but I notice they don't seem to fit. He says he has no toes. He tells me he froze them off.

He says he was working in the Laurentians one winter when he fell on some ice and hit his head. He woke up and crawled back to his house. He says a neighbour found him lying in the snow.

Yes, well. The point is, he has no toes but he has a decent pair of shoes. He has a room but the point is, he lives on the street. He doesn't read the papers, but the point is he's well read. Tennyson is his favourite poet. Mickey is a poet, too. What's a poet without contradictions?

The poet takes another drink.

His day is one long improvisation. He has no set routine, except for the liquor store at ten. He eats at drop-in centres, he walks wherever he wants to go, whenever he wants to go there. "Let's go," he says.

He ditches his smoke and gets up quickly, easily. The lack of toes gives him a forward, rolling gait. He looks like an optimist on foot. Then again, maybe it's the lithium. Mickey's a manic-depressive.

He says most of the guys on the street are on meds. He tells me he never gets sick. He says he rarely gets a cold. The vodka is a kind of medicine.

"Let's walk over to the university," he says. He likes to drink on campus. It's the intellectual atmosphere. He likes to be among people who use their heads.

There's a chill in the air. The kids on the street look fresh, as if they've just washed their faces and eaten their morning apples.

Suddenly we are ambushed by two men with a camera and a microphone. "We're journalists from Alberta," they say. "We want to know what you think about the referendum." Mickey keeps walking. The journalists hurry to keep up.

Mickey says everybody here gets along now that all the English have learned to speak French. He says separation's just a way for the business class of the Parti Quebecois to keep the money for themselves.

A Marxist analysis is more than the Albertans bargained for. They ask Mickey a bit about himself. He says he's half and half. The Albertans press him on the question of whether the French and English get along.

"Damn right we do," he says.

He ditches the journalists and heads up one of the streets of the campus. We pass the religious studies building. The entrance is grand, set back from the street and protected from the weather. Mickey tells me he wintered in this doorway one year when he had a sleeping bag.

In spite of the rootlessness, he seems connected here. He knows who he is, and I feel easy in his presence. This was not the always the case.

We met for the first time last week at the St. James United Church Drop-In Centre. He sized me up and looked around to see if anyone was watching.

"I've got a gun," Mickey said.

Pale light fell through stained glass windows. Half a dozen guys smoked cigarettes. Nobody looked anybody in the eye. Nobody talked, or looked at us.

I tried to keep calm. I watched a man spread processed cheese on a slice of bread. He licked the knife and put it on the counter. He slapped the slices of bread together. He took a bite of sandwich. He chewed furiously. He snuck a look.

I took a mental step backward.

Mickey grinned. "Don't worry," he said, patting his jacket pocket. "It's just vodka. I drink a mickey a day. I'm well known for that." Oh. So Mickey's a nickname.

"My street name," he said. "My real name's Phil."

Finally, we reached a patch of McGill campus lawn. "That's disgusting," he said. He pointed with his shoe to a dead bird lying on the grass. Two wasps, furtive as lovers, burrowed into the dead bird's neck.

Mickey looked away.

"You've got to go now. That's enough. I'd like to be by myself. Maybe I'll see you around." He walked towards a nearby tree.

Clothed with his breath, and looking, as he walk'd, larger than human on the frozen hills. He heard the deep behind him and a cry before.

Tennyson, Mickey's favourite. He lay down in a depression in the grass, pulled the bottle from his jeans, and took a drink. And waved goodbye. And watched until he was alone.

A NICKEL AT A TIME

It's eight-thirty in the morning in the middle of the week, and there is a line-up at the entrance to the supermarket in the food court of the Galeries du Parc.

It isn't a big line. There are only three people. But then, there are almost always three people and they're always carrying shopping bags.

They aren't shopping.

They have come in from the street. They are the ones who poke around barehanded in the garbage for the empty tins you throw away. You look away from them when you see them do this, and if they aren't yet hardened by what they do, they look away from you.

Now this morning, at the entrance to this supermarket, in front of a recycling machine, in the wake of men and women going to work, and in full view of people eating pastries in the café across the way, the can collectors are cashing in.

A nickel at a time.

First in line is a man in his late fifties. He wears work pants and a sweater. His sleeves are pushed up, his arms are deeply tanned. He has three big bags. He shoves his cans, one after another, into the recycling machine.

Behind him is an old woman wearing a car coat and a kerchief. And behind her is a thin man with a little potbelly, dressed in jeans and a T-shirt. He's in his forties, he has a bag of cans in each hand and an alkie smirk on his face.

The recycling machine looks like your fridge, except it's grey and twice as big. It inhales each can with an electronic *vweep*, and the man in the sweater jerks his hand away as if the machine had teeth.

It doesn't have teeth, it has rollers. The rollers crush the cans and the cans drop down, deep inside the guts of the fridge-like machine. *Vweep, vweep.*

When his bags are empty, the man with the rolled-up sleeves presses a button and the machine spits out a receipt. He takes the receipt to a cashier and she gives him some money. He had 171 cans. She gives him $8.55.

The woman with the kerchief has fewer cans, but she has two bags of bottles. She could be your old and dotty aunt. She walks away with four bucks and change.

Now a young kid comes out of the supermarket and steps in front of the alkie. He is wearing a dark apron, a white shirt and a tie, and he's pulling a shopping cart behind him like a wagon.

His hair looks water-combed. He slips a key in a lock and opens the door of the machine with a practised hand, as if he were getting a glass of milk. The alkie waits his turn. The liquor store won't be open for an hour.

Inside the machine is a large box lined with a heavy-duty plastic bag. The bag is filled with flattened cans. This machine crushes 12,000 cans a week.

The supermarket kid is in a hurry. He tries to lift the bag out of the box. At the same time, he tries to push the box back in the machine with his foot, and set the bag in the shopping cart.
No dice.

The box will not slide straight, the kid loses his balance, and the cans spill out of the top of the bag and fall on the floor. Not all of them. Only a couple of hundred.

The cans skitter and clatter on the tiles, flat as aluminum playing cards, each with a mind of its own. The alkie jumps out of the way. Shoppers look around for the cause of the commotion. Coffee-drinkers in the café peek over their morning papers.

Everybody grins.

The alkie reaches down and lends the boy a hand. When all the flattened cans are picked up off the floor, the boy lowers the bag into the shopping cart. The cart is completely full. The kid wheels it away.

People rush through the mall on their way to work. A girl bounces by in runners and tights, heading for the gym. An hour later she will walk back with a glowing face and a towel around her neck, the tip of her pony tail wet with sweat.

I finish my espresso. It costs me a buck and a half.

Thirty cans.

Now an old couple steps up to the machine. They are tiny, square and Mediterranean. He is wearing a blue hunting cap, the kind with ear flaps. He wears khaki pants, flat shoes and a blue suit jacket with pinstripes.

She is wearing a camel-coloured sweater. She has a thin gold band on the third finger of her right hand. Her hair is steely-grey, pulled tight on her head, secured at the back with a rubber band. She's wearing hard black shoes with athletic socks pulled up tight on her calves.

The man feeds the machine. *Vweep, vweep.* She sets two bags beside him, and sits on a bench to wait. He takes his receipt and gets his money, no more than a couple of bucks.

Now he sits across from her. They don't speak. After a time, they get up and walk a dozen paces down the mall. They sit down again on a bench. They seem tired, but they sit up straight. She keeps her hands in her lap. He sits with his hands on his knees, square and erect. He looks like a stone lion guarding a gate.

He reaches behind him and takes a skinny wallet from his pocket. He opens it up. Inside, I can see a five-dollar bill and a two-dollar bill. He lays the fresh deuce on top of the two bills, and puts the wallet back in his pants.

He and his wife sit without saying a word. And on some signal which I do not see, they get up and walk away.

SUMMER ISN'T OVER
UNTIL THE MAN GETS OFF HIS STILTS

I've been watching the skies reluctantly for strings of geese. Last night I wore a sweater in the house, and when I went to the dépanneur for a quart of two percent at ten p.m., I blew puffs of milky breath. Today I'll get a pumpkin at the market and bring it home with a turkey and half a dozen ears of Indian corn.

Just don't tell me it's Thanksgiving.

The leaves may be changing colour and dropping like flies, but summer isn't over until Greg Dunleavy sheds his saxophone and takes up winter quarters in the métro with his flute.

Greg dances on stilts and plays snatches of standards for quarters on Ste. Catherine. Down the street from him, a band of South Americans is strumming hard to stay warm. The cold is hard on their hands, but they have an advantage over Greg. They can work the crowds in ponchos. It's part of who they are.

Greg's arms are bare. He works in blue cotton pants with six-foot legs, with a purple pirate scarf on his head, a pink sash at his waist and a blue tank top. It's part of who he is.

He moves with all the grace of a giraffe, if a giraffe could pirouette in clothes like that and play the sax. Greg is nine feet tall. No giraffe I know of has ever danced for quarters on Ste. Catherine. Step. Dip. Kick.

It may be too cold for giraffes, but it's not too cold for Greg. Not yet. He's lean and in good shape for his fifty-plus years. Confidence is attractive, don't you think?

Greg's eyes are squinty and flinty and full of predatory appraisal, which is not surprising when you learn he's been a harness maker, and a peacekeeper in the Congo, and that he once supplemented his table by foraging for wild plants.

You learn to make appraisals when you're staring up the backside of a horse or down the barrel of a gun, or across a plate of supper dandelions.

Greg wears elbow pads in case he falls. He's confident but he's not stupid. He fell once and he doesn't want to fall again. A fall is dangerous when you're nine feet tall. Step. Dip. Kick.

He plays the sax well enough to plant a tune that takes root like a weed in the heads of passers-by. Grab your coat and get your hat. It isn't winter yet. You can't plant a tune on frozen ground.

Greg sees everything from up there—camcorders and prams and kids on bikes or rollerblades. Leave your worries on the doorstep.

Step. Dip. Sway. Kick.

A woman tries to take a photograph. Just direct your feet. "Excuse me, ma'am. If you want to take a picture, please leave something for the artist." She reaches into her handbag. Step. Dip. Step. She fishes out some coins and drops them on the sunny side of the street.

Two kids push their way through the gathered crowd. They are young and in love. They can't stop laughing, hugging and touching each other all over. His hair is twice as long as hers and dirty, and he wears his baseball cap backwards.

When they see Greg, the boy gets on his knees. The girl is shy and reluctant, but the boy insists, and then he sticks his neck between her legs and lifts her up. And he becomes her stilts, and suddenly she's tall enough to dance with Greg. Step. Dip.

And then the young man dances down the sidewalk with the girl, and then he sets her down, and they walk down the street touching each other some more.

As long as kids can still do that, it's summer.

For now, on a busy weekend afternoon, the sidewalks are crowded with shoppers and strollers, and Greg clears a fifteen-foot circle around himself. The tiny stilt feet look graceful but lethal. You must remember this. A kiss is just a step, dip, kick.

Two men, nearly seven feet tall themselves, pass by. For them, a man on stilts is just another man. A sigh is just a sigh. One of the tall men snaps a photo. The fundamental things apply.

Greg calls to the two tall men. If you want to take a picture, you have to pay the artist. They pay no heed. The artist follows them for half a block, pointing at them with his sax. The effect is disconcerting. Shoppers turn their heads to see what happens. I turn mine. I would not want an angry, nine-foot pirate of a giraffe on my tail.

The artist loses this one at the lights.

But the world will always welcome lovers and nine-foot men who dip and sway and dance with saxophones. You can't do that in winter.

Soon, it will be too cold to play an instrument on the sidewalk. Any day now, the South American musicians are going to move indoors. None of that matters. Don't tell me this is Thanksgiving weekend. I'm not listening. It's still summer as long as Greg is out there, standing tall as time goes by.

TATTOO YOU

The bald kid on the métro got my attention.

Shaved heads aren't unusual these days, given the endurance of neo-fascism and the presence in our midst of fashion refugees, but this kid stood out from the pack. He had the letters "SKINH" tattooed high across his forehead, where his hairline might have been. The penmanship was bad.

There was only one question to ask.

Then I noticed he was sitting forward in his seat, clenching and unclenching his fists, glancing everywhere and nowhere all at once. He looked like he was tired of answering questions, asked or unasked. I kept my mouth shut and my gaze indirect. Fortunately, I have good peripheral vision.

I wanted to know which way he was going, and I don't mean Angrignon.

Was he making his way, one letter at a time, towards "SKINHEAD?" Or had he grown tired of "SKINHEAD," and was he in the middle of the painful process of subtracting a letter at a time, in the hopes of leaving himself a clean slate and a clean pate?

I didn't have the nerve to ask.

I can't get him out of my mind. His tattoo is the most extreme act of self-reference and self-loathing I've ever seen. As someone who tends to see the world in fluctuating shades of grey, I can't think of a single image or slogan, no matter how attractively inked, that I'd want to commit myself to forever.

I seem to be alone.

There are tattoos all over the lot, some of them startlingly good and some of them simply startling. In the past few weeks, I've spotted tiny ink tears etched below the eyes of guys who don't look like they've wept in quite a while.

I've seen slave bracelets drawn to resemble barbed wire on a variety of ankles. I've seen roses on the crests of young girl's breasts, and cartoon characters inked on pale old arms where some others of us bear the scarified marks of vaccination. I've seen those old standbys "LOVE" and "HATE" on the knuckles of thugs.

I presume they were Anglo thugs.

But if you think Skinh's badly-lettered and unfortunately-placed tattoo lumps him in with the lumpenproletariat, you should consider the repugnance of Roseanne's rear, or take a look at the thing on Cher's left arm.

The most famous Montreal tattoo is the one sported by Eve Salvail, the model with the drop-dead pout and the Shaolin dragon upside her head. Eve was smart—okay, not real smart, but smarter than my pal Skinh. She put her tattoo where, when she lets her hair grow out, none of the rest of us have to see it.

Here's the thing about tattoos—whether they arise from vanity or rage, they are at once blatant and forbidden, and the indelible price of admission to a club most of us will never join. That's why kids do it.

How exclusive is this club? There is a museum in Japan where you can display your tattooed hide after you've died, Clyde. Let me make that clearer. This museum contains the real, full-body skins of actual former humans. It's a set-up which would have made Lydia the Tattooed Lady feel at home.

Her, and my son Matt. We got together a couple of weeks ago. My son and I, that is. We hadn't seen each other for a couple of years. It had taken that long to cool off. We went through his teens like a pair of Shermans burning down the each other's South. Our civil war's over now, thank God.

I picked him up at the airport and brought him home. Hugs all around, and everyone glad. And then he sat back and crossed his legs, and I noticed his tattoos. He had a replica of the world's largest living lizard on his left leg. And a bolt of forked, black lightning ran the length of his right calf.

Yikes.

Whoever inked them in had stayed inside the lines. But my son, for pete's sake. My baby boy, the kid whose only other identifying mark is a mole on his upper lip, in the same place as the mole on mine. I kept my mouth shut. Done is done.

There have been other tattoos in my family. My uncle Frank had a rose and scroll on his forearm, the kind of display piece not uncommon on men of a certain generation who went to the lakes in ships. But Frank stopped at his forearm. At least, I think he did. Only my late Aunt Josie knew for sure.

I have no idea how far my son Matt is going to go. It's his business. But at least with leg tattoos, if the boss invites him over for a pool party years from now, he has an option. He can jump in fully clothed. Or he can smile and say he can't swim.

My friend Skinh has fewer choices.

On his behalf I had a chat with Keith Stewart, the big needle at Artistic Tattooing. Keith rolled his eyes. He won't tattoo a face. He said there was hope for Skinh. Keith said he's removed tattoos using an inkless tattoo needle. It's a process he described as "chopping up the meat and then salting it." He meant real salt. By meat, he meant flesh. He said it takes months to complete and he said it hurts like hell.

I believe him.

I also believe it leaves a scar. But Keith also said ruby laser therapy does the job. That's the same technology used to remove port wine stains. It's expensive, but there are doctors in town who can do it.

Skinh, if you're reading this, you should know you have a choice. You can see a doctor. You can talk to Keith.

Or you can get yourself a ski mask.

A LITTLE COFFEE TALK IN THE MALL
WITH THE PRINCE ARTHUR BOYS

I'll tell you about the The Prince Arthur Boys, although I should tell you first that they have too much bare scalp, they own too many partial plates, and there have been too many notches let out of their belts for them to be considered boys.

But they have been friends, rough and smooth, for sixty years. They have remained friends since they were boys.

They started off, immigrants and the sons of immigrants, near the corner of Prince Arthur and the Main. They grew up together, left school together, endured poverty and war, watched each other's children grow, shared victories, drinks and defeats. They can look at each other to this day and remember the boys that they were.

Their friendship is bound with a long cord of talk, beaded like a rosary with names and dates and places. The stories they tell are repetitive and comforting as prayers.

The Boys meet every afternoon in a coffee shop in a shopping plaza in the north end of the city. They've been doing this for the past three years.

Dyno Don and Johnny Savick came up with the idea to meet on a regular basis. They pay dues like the members of a club, and fines for offences real and imagined. There are nearly two dozen Boys. They fine each other frequently. Fines are paid in brandy. They like their coffee spiked.

They went to Aberdeen School when they were young. They fiddled in class while Miss Hecht burned. They obeyed Mr. Wilkinson, the dreaded and beloved Wilkie, who ruled over them with a sound knowledge of boys and the help of a stick called Slapitus.

They graduated from Aberdeen, thanks to Slapitus. And they graduated from the Prince Arthur Academy with the help of a stick of a different sort—the Academy was a pool room. These Boys know pool tables and times tables; they can handle nine eights and nine balls with equal ease. They know how to size up a stranger and, thanks to Wilkie, they still know when it isn't safe to run a hustle.

The names of The Boys are legends, polished hard as stone:

Zimmie Junior is a dapper man with a clipped moustache and silver hair. He used to play soccer; he still has a runner's trimness. He was a conscientious objector during the war. It was a badge of courage. He spent the war in a camp for conscientious objectors, running all day long with a loaded pack on his back. Whenever the subject of running comes up, the Prince Arthur Boys say "Zimmie knows running."

They say this, and he hears it, with a kind of awe. Did it really happened so long ago, and did it happen to Zimmie?

Damn right it did.

So long ago.

Savick played semi-pro ball for the Pirates in the old days. He might have made it all the way, but he broke his leg, his collarbone, his fingers. Sav walks gingerly now, the way old athletes walk. You can see, in the way he walks, how good he could have been.

The Hook reminds you of your wife's uncle. He is a quiet man, and you figure you could trust him if you had to. He has regular features. I've no idea why they call him The Hook. But today, the coffee has been spiked.

There is a chorus of explanations:

"The Hook used to have a beak." "We knew a guy in the old days called The Beak, but The Beak had nothing on The Hook." "The Hook put Dick Tracy to shame."

The Hook is silent, forbearing.

He's heard all this before. He's heard it all his life. Even though he had a nose job forty years ago, even though his nose today is what you might call pert, he's still The Hook.

Jimmy the Wop, a large man with bad knees and a big smile, is the Latin Lover of the group. He has just been admitted back into the ranks in good standing. See, Jimmy was missing for over a week. He never called the others, never said if he was sick or where he was. Jimmy's girlfriend's family was in town. A man has obligations. So does a Prince Arthur Boy. The fine was a forty-pounder of brandy.

Welcome back, Jimmy.

Little Joe's job is to call the meetings to order, to preside over the daily court, to keep track of the dues. He's in charge of pouring shots under the table, and proposing toasts as necessary.

U-Boat hasn't paid his dues for a while. They call him U-Boat because he's German, and when he was a kid he used to swim under the dock of the yacht club, and you get the picture. U-boat pays two-thirds of his fine, and ponies up a two-ounce bottle of slivovitz. He takes a ribbing for his two ounces of generosity.

Isn't that tricky, I ask, drinking out loud? Oh, we keep it discreet, say the Boys. We look after the waitress. We don't let things get out of hand.

The afternoon wears on, softens at the edges.

The Boys look like your dad a year or two after he retired. They were managers and foremen, men who worked hard all their lives. Now they meet to pass the time and pool their dues; they buy lottery tickets, they spike their coffee, and talk.

Stories fly of Blinder the Pickpocket, a man with Coke-bottle glasses who picked a pocket and then had his own pocket picked; of games of football played with a stuffed stocking; and of a guy from the old days who ran with the wrong crowd and was found cut up in pieces in a field.

"Hey," says Little Joe. "You see that woman over there? You see her? Take a look at her. Look at her eyes." There's something familiar about her, all right. She has a tight little smile and coal-black eyes. "That's Rocket Richard's sister. She was tougher than he was."

Shoppers prowl the mall, drifting in and out of view with their string bags full of bargains, unaware of any guys who were cut up.

Unaware of The Rocket's sister.

Andy, who I've come to think of as Andy With No Nickname, leaves to run an errand. The Shadow makes his appearance later in the day. He stays off to the side and in the background, as if he were a shadow in a picture of the boys taken on a summer long ago.

Finally the time for supper comes. There are wives at home, grandchildren to babysit. The Prince Arthur Boys get up slowly, stiffly, and call it a day.

You might call it a life.

THE SEPTEMBER OF A BALLPLAYER

The catcher was a Romanian-born Serb who grew up in Montreal. A hot prospect, he could run, he could hit for power, he had a gun for an arm and a head for the game. All he needed was a nickname.

Naturally, they called him "Eskimo."

Johnny Savick played Class "D" baseball in the late forties and early fifties. He is a rawhide-looking man with a wide chest, an open face, a confident nose. He is the unlikeliest-looking Eskimo you ever saw, but you figure he's a catcher as soon as you look at his hands.

Last Sunday, we were sitting in the ballpark watching the Expos and the Mets. Ever the craftsman, Savick watches the Expos' catcher, Tim Laker. "See the way he protects himself." Laker squats to take a pitch, and tucks his throwing hand behind his knee. Savick holds his own hand out. Each thick finger points in a different direction. The thumb is gnarled, bent back at an unnatural angle.

He didn't protect himself enough.

In fact, he is a mountain range of broken bones—there is a lump where his collarbone meets his shoulder, his right ankle is permanently swollen, and he walks like a man whose shoes are filled with shards of glass.

This, for the love of sport.

The Expos come to the plate in the bottom of the first inning. David Segui drives in a run with a tidy double, and Berry singles him home. A promising start. Mike Lansing is greeted with half-hearted boos, the consequence of some intemperate remarks about the language debate made earlier in the week. He turns the boos to half-hearted cheers with a single.

When the inning ends, it's two-zip, Expos.

Savick has always played. As a kid, he and the Prince Arthur boys used to dig a hole under the fence at Mont St. Louis College and play ball on the diamond there. Now and then, he'd smash a window with a long ball.

One day a brother—this was an athletic man, a brother as fleet as the wind—caught them before they could run away. He issued a challenge: if Savick and his chums could beat the kids on the college team, the brother would spring for chocolate milk and Mae Wests all around.

"Chocolate milk? No way we were going to lose."

How good was Johnny Savick?

In his teens, he made $12.00 a week playing ball in the Montreal major junior league; this, during the Depression. If you don't think that was a big deal, you should know he was making 25¢ an hour as an apprentice in a machine shop at the time.

Now the inning dies, and the sound system in the stadium pumps out some vaguely familiar music. There is a lion in a tuxedo walking down one of the aisles. A girl in a wedding dress clings to his arm. Beauty and the Beast at the ballgame. They don't stay long. Who can blame them? The Expos give up five runs in the third.

Could Savick have made it to the majors?

His career had a promising beginning in the Pittsburgh organization, and a spectacular, if premature, end. After he broke his collarbone playing for the Mount Vernon Kings, he healed up and got a second chance—the Pirates sent him to play for Greenville in the Ohio Valley League.

The weather was lousy on the day of Johnny's last game. There was a strong wind blowing in from the outfield. It looked like a tornado brewing. The teams played anyway. That's life in the minors.

During the game, an opposing player hit a towering home run. The ball was headed for the outfield fence until the wind picked it up and threw it back in the field of play. What looked like a home run dropped in Savick's mitt in front of the plate.

Nice catch, Eskimo.

Later in the game, with the wind blowing harder, Savick hit a long single. He got the go-ahead to steal second on the next pitch. When he glanced down the line, he saw a funnel cloud; cars from an amusement park were flying through the air as if a giant child were throwing a tantrum with his toys.

Field of Dreams, all right.

Bad ones.

People were inching out of the bleachers with their eyes on the storm when Sav stole second. He slid in hard. The storm broke just as his ankle did. He remembers lying on the ground with the rain falling in his face. That was the end of his career.

Tough luck, Eskimo.

Now an Expo sends a foul tip zipping past our heads. It's too far away to stab at, but it's close enough that I can hear it spinning thickly in the dead air of the stadium.

Somebody in the stands starts a desultory wave. "Looks like the tide's out," says Sav. Paid attendance is announced as thirteen thousand.

If it is, I'm an Eskimo myself.

During the seventh inning stretch, a team of pretty girls from a cosmetics company urges us to exercise. Claudia Schiffer pouts and thrusts her stadium-sized bosom out from the scoreboard screen. The music is pumping, hypnotic and sexual.

A fat security guy stares at the backside of one of the exercise girls. You can tell she isn't happy shaking her booty in his face, but a girl's got to make a living, and some people actually wave their arms in a parody of exercise.

They look like they are fighting an attack of bees.

Sav digs me in the ribs with an elbow. "Look at this," he says. There is a small boy in front of us. He is too short to see the girls in their leotards, and too young to understand what Claudia is selling. But he's dancing for everything he's worth.

He's four years old.

When you're four, you dance.

Mark Grudzielanek steps up to the plate in the eighth inning. The young shortstop taps the plate with his bat, and spreads his legs wide. He flies to right for an easy out. "He's got a four-inch stride. That's as far as he's going to hit the ball with a stance like that," says Savick. The four-year-old kid agrees and falls asleep with his mouth open. Sav smiles a grandfatherly smile.

His mind is not on the game. Does he ever dream about playing ball? "I don't dream. When my head hits the pillow, I'm out for the night. Anyway, there's no point looking back. In life, you have to look ahead."

Our heroes have no choice but to look ahead. They die meekly in the bottom of the ninth, and disappear with their tails between their legs while the Mets trade high-fives on the mound.

Sav gets up stiffly from his seat, and snorts. You can tell he thinks the Expos would play better if they were a little bit hungry. How hungry? Hungry enough to play for a Mae West and a chocolate milk.

THE CHAMP IS FIGHTING FOR HIS WIFE

Lou Alter is small, slight and exceedingly fit for a man in his seventies. He has wispy hair, thick glasses and the distorted hands of a retired prize fighter. He is what they used to call a sharp dresser. He is marking a pair of anniversaries this month.

Fifty-one years ago today, Lou stepped into a boxing ring in New York City and fought a young man from Boston named Sandy Saddler. It was the second time in a week the two had faced each other with intent.

Saddler would go on to become the featherweight champion of the world, tenth on *Ring* magazine's list of all-time champs in his weight class, pound for pound a legend among the little men who practise the most brutal of sports.

Alter won the first match hands down.

He won the second fight, too, although it's in the record books as a draw. Lou Alter mutters something under his breath about the New York clique, but he won't say more than that. Boxing was, and is, a dirty business.

The second anniversary hurts more than the first.

Last June, Lou's wife Ruth had a stroke.

She's been in the hospital ever since, speechless and without much movement in the right side of her body. Physiotherapy would help, but the doctors at the hospital were reluctant to make such a recommendation.

This has been tougher than anything Lou faced in the ring. He is, however, a patient man. You don't get to be the champ by quitting when you're in a corner. Lou jabbed at the doctors for a year. He went to the hospital every day. He told the doctors all Ruth needed was a little physio.

Two weeks ago, he shamed them into agreement.

Ruth started therapy, and now the hospital is teaching Lou how to help her work out. It's slow going. It doesn't matter. Ruth is the love of his life. Lou visits her daily, spends every evening with her, talks to her even though all she can do is squeeze his hand weakly, and look at him with loving eyes.

Lou calls the hospital every morning, to make sure she's all right. When he is assured, he takes a daily coffee with friends at a doughnut shop near his house.

He meet the same guys every day—Freddie who sells T-shirts, Dick who owns a small chain of restaurants, Phil who volunteers at the veterans' hospital, and a few other guys, all good guys, friends.

After coffee, Lou works out at a gym in a mall. It is not a boxer's gym—there's no speedbag and no spitting, no smell of sweat and liniment and blood. Instead, there are carpets on the floor and rock music in the air.

And everywhere you look there are young women with aphrodite pony tails. The women smell of soap. They trot stylishly on treadmills. Bright spandex seems painted on the hard curves of their bodies.

Lou runs in their midst with a steady stride. But there is something in the air, a dissonance of sorts. The women do not seem to know what to make of a skinny old man who packs more testosterone in his shorts than a bar full of bikers on Saturday night.

Lou runs for half an hour, looking out the window onto the sidewalk of the mall. He runs the way a boxer runs, bobbing and weaving, jabbing the air with a quick left, left that startles passers-by. He weighs one hundred and five pounds, but there's enough power behind his hands to stun a man twice his size.

After six miles on the treadmill, Lou drops to the floor and does leg lifts, then he hits the exercise machines for work on his arms and his chest, his legs and his back and his neck. Boys building their bodies envy him.

After a shower, Lou takes lunch.

Today, he goes for a burger at his friend Dick Potenza's restaurant. The burgers are good. There are sports memorabilia on the walls. Dick knows his customers by name. We sit in a booth beneath a picture of the man who held the Canadian featherweight championship from 1947 to 1950.

You can't tell from the picture that Lou Alter is a little man.

His chest is wide as a city street. He has shoulders that won't quit. That's where the punching power comes from, the shoulders. He has eyes that look right through you. In the photo as in life.

Lou and Dick have something in common. They are men with big hearts who have had grand love affairs. With their wives.

Dick says about Ann, "I visit her at the cemetery every day. She's the love of my life. On Fridays, I bring flowers, two red roses."

Ann's been gone seven years. Dick says, "Young couples come into this restaurant holding hands. I tell them life is short."

Lou nods his head and says, "I go to the hospital every day and tell Ruth how much I love her. I tell her I miss her. I call her sweetheart, and I ask her when she's coming home."

The table is silent for a moment.

Ruth Alter never cared much for boxing. She met Lou after he quit the ring. Alas, quitting the ring didn't mean quitting fights. After he hung up the gloves, Lou Alter tended bar in east end Montreal.

One night a six-foot loudmouth was getting rowdy, making trouble, stabbing the little man's chest with a thick finger. Lou said, "Come on, you've had enough. Tomorrow's another day."

The big man said he wanted to fight. He said he'd wait for Lou outside. Lou said he wouldn't have long to wait. Lou took off his apron.

There was nobody waiting outside. Lou figured the big guy was hiding around the corner with a sucker punch, so he approached the side of the building carefully. Sure enough, the hulk was in the shadows.

The big man swung. Lou ducked and stepped inside and levelled the blowhard with a short right to the stomach. The big man crumpled and stayed down. When the cops arrived, they looked at Lou. They looked at the big man on the ground. And then they shook their heads and hauled the big man away.

None of that now. Not any more.

Lou quit all that for Ruth. She was smart, though, picking a fighter. Even though the hands that hold hers tonight are boxer's hands, crumpled from the force of old blows, they are still strong.

Lou's holding on to her for life.

AFTER A BRIEF DELAY,
TRAFFIC ON THE VILLE MARIE IS BACK TO NORMAL

You can tell something is terribly wrong. There are a dozen people standing outside the Place d'Armes métro, peering into the Ville Marie tunnel. Usually, nobody stands here. It's too dirty, too noisy, too dark.

Someone points down below; most days at noon there are hundreds of cars streaking by on their way to who knows where. There is no traffic now. There are five cop cars and there is a fire truck with flashing lights. There are a couple of idle rescue trucks. There is a Magnus Poirier van.

Whatever it is, it's serious.

Cops pace and point and scribble notes on pads. Firemen stand with their hands on their hips. A cop takes off his cap and scratches his head the way a man does when there's nothing to be done.

And then you see.

A little black car is impossibly wedged under the back end of a red flat-bed truck. The top of the car is crumpled, peeled back like a box top. The tail end of the flat-bed had sheared it away. Someone has draped a yellow tarpaulin over the driver's seat of the car.

Now there are two dozen people gawking. We peer over the rough edges of the concrete wall outside the métro, and they point down into the tunnel. Those who've been watching the longest show new arrivals where to look.

A middle-aged woman, dressed for work at the office, approaches carefully so as not to dirty her dress. She looks at me quizzically. I shake my head. She decides to look anyway. She puts her fingers against the wall and leans forward and peers down. And then she puts her hand over her mouth and walks away.

A man in a short-sleeved shirt hurries up to the wall. He has a little boy's grin on his face. A traffic accident—how stupid for them, how lucky for me! When he realizes what would have had to happen for the car to get like that, he stops smiling.

Down below, a man spreads a bag of sand over something which has spilled from the little black car. I look away. I notice a spider web shrouded carelessly against one of the ridges in the concrete wall. When I look down again, the windshield of the little car looks like a shroud.

Three cops with clipboards kneel by the back end of the flat-bed truck. They point here and there, they shine flashlights underneath, looking for a way to free the torn black car.

A woman in a summer dress brings her two kids near. She puts her cigarette between her lips and lifts her kids in her arms so they can have a look. I tell her she might not want to let them see. She pouts, pushes the cigarette forward with her lips. She is thinking to herself that I should mind my own business. She says the kids aren't old enough to understand.

Emergency lights spin silently, painting intermittent streaks of colour on the shirts of the men. You want to hear sirens. You want to see someone hurry. You want a little hope. There is no hope. The men are taking their time. I look down, and all I can think of is falling.

Finally, a tow truck backs into place. A man hitches a cable to the bumper of the car. Forty people watch the cable tighten. Nothing happens. And then the black car frees itself with a shudder. A man stands next to me, squinting through his camcorder. He has a camcorder grin on his face.

A fireman adjusts the yellow tarp; it is a delicate gesture, as if he were tucking a blanket around a child on a cold night. Another fireman reaches in and puts some papers in a plastic bag. No one looks into the car unless he has to.

The Magnus Poirier men wear short-sleeved shirts and ties in the heat. They snap white rubber gloves on their hands. They spread a white plastic sheet on a stretcher. They pause a moment, and then they reach into the black car and carefully raise the tarpaulin and tug at something limp.

"I don't envy that family now," says a woman at my side. "When you leave your house in the morning, you better pray to Jesus you'll be safe. Oh, this hurts," she says.

The cops take more measurements. The black car is winched onto a tow truck and then it is strapped down and hauled away. The Magnus Poirier men strap something limp and heavy onto their stretcher. They peel off their gloves and speak for a moment with the police. And then they, too, drive away.

A man in a red safety vest sweeps up the spilled sand. Three men in red vests watch him work. Next to me, a man in sunglasses shakes his head and says, "A human life, just like that." He looks at me sadly. "Have a nice day," he says.

The cops take final measurements.

Now there is no one left up above because there is nothing left to see. The sand on the road has been swept aside. All the emergency vehicles have gone. A single cop car leads the first wave of traffic through the tunnel. In its midst is a small black car, another flat-bed truck.

Slowly at first, but ever faster, traffic comes up to speed.

EVERY DAY THERE IS A PARADE OF MIRACLES
AT ST. JOSEPH'S ORATORY

Alphérie Plante was an engineer for CP Rail. One day he was working on some track when a piece of metal flew up and lodged in his right eye. His left eye was already very weak. Suddenly he was almost blind. Disaster loomed.

He had nine children to support. Monsieur Plante was desperate. The doctor was no use. His wife Alma, a practical woman, said "Alphérie, why don't you go to Montreal to see Brother André?"

Brother André couldn't hurt.

Alphérie rode to Montreal. He stood patiently in line, waiting for a chance to speak with the little healer. When his turn came, Brother André rubbed some holy oil on Alphérie's eye and gave him a medal of St. Joseph. He told Alphérie to make a novena, and told him to go home. "That's all?" wondered Alphérie Plante. Brother André shooed him away.

By the time he reached home, the railroad man was back on the tracks. His eye had healed. Julie Plante, Alphérie's granddaughter, tells this story happily. She is a tour guide at St. Joseph's Oratory. Her story makes the place seem real.

She is about to lead the first tour of the day when three older men in short-sleeved shirts and straw hats rush to her side. They are out of breath. Priests in mufti. "We're from Texas," they say. "We just drove 2,500 miles to get here. We'd like to say a quick mass." Julie makes a call. A quick mass it is.

All in a day's work.

Julie's first tour group is made up of forty elderly Americans. I tag along. She tells us the story of Brother André's vocation, tells us how this little illiterate man was able to accomplish miracles of healing with a faith that was both simple and obstinate.

She also tells us of the stomach trouble which plagued him all his life. Brother André would have felt at home in this group of sufferers. "My carotids are fine," a woman says emphatically to a friend. "A bit of urinary incontinence," whispers a man. Another woman says, "Blood clots. I died three years ago on the operating table." She raises a pant leg and shows a companion her knee. It is swollen badly.

Julie leads us past André's crypt.

An elderly woman asks, for the fourth time, how old Brother André was when he died. He lived to be 91 years old, says Julie with a smile. A woman whispers, not so *sotto voce,* "She keeps asking the same question."

Another woman asks to speak. Julie smiles again. Some of these pilgrims have their own agenda. The woman says her father lived to the age of 99, and her mother to 93, and they were married 75 years.

Everyone is smiling now.

I detach myself and watch a young sacristan named Risée. He is replacing votive candles in front of a statue. That's his job, replacing candles. That's all he does, from morning to night. How many candles? "Let's see," he says, "I go through 20 boxes of little candles every day. There are 250 candles in each box. And I use 90 boxes of big candles , and there are 18 of those in each box." Risée smiles as if he doesn't quite believe it.

Outside, a young woman in a skimpy dress and high heels totters by a set of stairs which leads directly to the church. She stops to read a sign. "These steps are reserved for pilgrims who climb up on their knees." The young woman grimaces. There are more than a hundred steps. Who'd do such a thing?

Many people do such a thing. I ask a woman from Syracuse why she's going up the hard way. Her voice breaks. She says her mother is very ill, and her mother-in-law has cancer. She has a simple faith, a simple need of faith.

The parking lot fills with tour buses. I notice a bronze Jaguar and a white stretch limo among them. I have no idea why the swells are here. Simply praying for more money, I guess.

An elderly priest from New Jersey stops to say hello. He's brought a group from his parish. He's been coming here for six or seven years. Not bad, I say. That's nothing, he says. There's a woman with his group who's made the trip every year for the last 44 years. I raise my eyebrows. He laughs and says, "I did the same when she told me."

Tourists come here from further afield than New Jersey. There is a group of Poles making a triple-header pilgrimage, stopping first at the Oratory, then heading for Cap de la Madeleine and Ste. Anne de Beaupré. There are also Swiss and Sri Lankans, Indians and Italians. There are Buddhists, Hindus, and Muslims, people of all races, all colours, all faiths.

Everyone stops at the gift shop.

It is a necessary evil, an embarrassment and a source of badly needed revenue, with bins of holy auto visor clips, holy fridge magnets, holy key rings, holy paper weights and pencils. You can buy a trick pen with a tiny St. Joseph who floats in front of a tiny Oratory—this is the same technology used in those pens where, when you tip them, a woman's skirt flies up.

You can buy thousands of medals of saints: Jude and Gerard, Martin and Blaise, Carmel and Theresa, Anthony and Francis, Bernadette and Benoit. St. Joseph is the big seller, naturally.

You can buy rosaries in white or blue or black or pink, green or yellow or red, made of wood or plastic or glass. You can even buy mini-rosaries with 10 Hail Mary's instead of the usual 50. I buy some medals and a bust of Brother André.

Brother André, the man who called himself St. Joseph's little dog, has been beatified—credited with two miracles. He needs one more to make sainthood. The church is looking for the third miracle now. I'm thinking if André could pull off a show like this, they're going to find it.

Five women in bright saris pass by on their way home for supper. The saris are the colour of rosaries. Julie smiles, but she looks tired. She has one more tour before the end of her day.

I ask her what the high point of her day has been. She says there was a woman in one of the groups who stayed close, said nothing, and wept quietly all the way through the tour. Finally, the woman approached Julie. She said her young son had recently died of cancer. She said the visit to the Oratory had given her strength.

That's miracle enough for me.

ROSES AND RESPONSIBILITIES

In the mountains of central Italy, in the province of Molise, there is a little village draped against an ancient hill. From the height of land, stone houses spill towards a valley lined with poppies and edged with trees.

From a distance, the hillside seems to have the sloping posture of a shoulder. The village is an epaulet of twelfth century stone houses whose walls are three feet thick.

Ripabottoni.

It is a tiny village. And although the valley is fertile and the field is yellow with grain, there's never been enough land to support everyone who wanted to live there. At times there has been terrible poverty. Many people have had to leave unwillingly. Many people won't say why they left.

My grandfather ended up in Northern Ontario.

He never said why he left.

Four thousand Montrealers have roots in Ripabottoni. They are a sociable and civic-minded group. Every spring, they hold an Italian sugaring-off party. Every summer they hold a picnic. Every November they hold an annual dinner and choose a young woman to embody the dreams of the old village in a new land.

They choose Miss Ripabottoni.

This year, the dinner is held in one of those marble-and-mirror banquet halls in the heart of St. Leonard. The ceiling of the hall is draped with white tulle, and a red and green satin banner hangs behind the bandstand. The banner is decorated with a single rose and the words "Comune di Ripabottoni."

I think immediately of my grandfather.

Matteo Fiorito left Ripabottoni more than a hundred years ago. He died before I was born and all his children—my dad, my aunts and uncles, a dozen of them—were born in Canada.

"You remind me of him," my father told me once.

The words were magical, and filled me with a puzzled delight. I never knew my grandfather, and I was hungry for the knowledge of family as I was growing up. But our family history is made of stories from the recent past and the present tense.

The hall begins to fill with broad-shouldered, hardworking couples. Short, strong people, built close to the ground. All the men look as if they know how to make wine and cut stone and grow flowers. They look as if they could handle a mule and slaughter a pig.

All the women have a steady gaze, and the kind of self-knowledge earned from a lifetime of hard work shared with family and friends. Their children are polite, and they kiss their aunts and cousins on both cheeks.

These people know who they are.

In their good clothes and their polished shoes, they also know they are better off here than they would have been had they stayed in Ripabottoni. There is a kind of sadness in this knowledge.

The old men look like pictures of my grandfather.

When my uncles spoke of Ripabottoni, if they spoke of it at all, it was simply to repeat a small handful of half-remembered stories. They told these stories the same way with every telling, so as not to lose the tiniest of details.

The story of the stolen butchered lamb.

The wagon-load of grain on the road to the mill on the hot and sunny day.

The horsewhip and the pistol.

The memories are fading. My aunts and uncles are in their eighties and they don't remember much any more. My little dad, the baby of the family, is seventy-seven. He isn't well these days. He's in Northern Ontario. I'm here.

He and I are running out of time.

When I call him on the phone, I sometimes surprise him with questions about my grandfather when he isn't expecting to hear them, in the hope that a sudden question will jar loose a detail.

No luck lately.

Supper is served, and it's what I eat at home. Antipasto. Chicken broth with acini di pepe. Penne rigate and ravioli. Then a salad, then a grilled steak with vegetables.

As we eat, a cheer goes up.

Five elderly couples step onto the dance floor in the traditional costume of Molise. The men wear knee-length breeches and white socks tied with red cord. The women wear long skirts and ruffled shirts. They wear red scarves tied loosely at their necks.

The dancers snap their fingers and clap their hands in a series of intricate and ancient patterns. The room fills with applause at the sight of a tiny white-haired couple. They are in their seventies. She moves gracefully, like a ship in slow water. He capers around her like a dolphin.

I went to Ripabottoni this summer. I was looking for stories to tell my father. I was greeted like a long-lost son. The people of the village showed me the house where my grandfather was born. They dug through crumbling ledgers and found a hundred and fifty years of family records. They made copies of these, and gave me gifts to give to my dad.

I found no relatives, but in the cemetery, I saw all the family names. Fiorito. Delvecchio. DiFabio. Silvaggio. This is who you are, said the people of Ripabottoni.

They gave me gifts and stole my heart and sent me home again.

After supper, waiters deliver fresh fruit to every table. The band delivers pop songs, folk music, standards from the Frank Sinatra songbook. Alda Viero, last year's president of the Association of Families of Ripabottoni, says, "You wait here. I'm going to find you another Joe Fiorito."

I don't believe her.

But she disappears in the crowded room and re-emerges to deliver a man my age. He is one of these solid-looking men, with a big grin on his face. He wants to say hello. He reaches to shake my hand.

"Joe Fiorito, meet Joe Fiorito."

It is late in the evening. Ties and tongues have loosened. The two Joes have made a date to look at family pictures. We may be cousins. We must be cousins. I hope we're cousins.

Now Mary Carmosino takes up her position on the bandstand. She is a charming woman who speaks English with her friends and French with her family. She speaks Italian to the crowd. She introduces us to Miss Ripabottoni of 1995.

Miss Ripabottoni is Tania Ciarla.

Her job is to represent the ideals of the tiny village from which most of these people have come. My grandfather's village.

Joe Fiorito's village.

Tania Ciarla takes a walk of honour around the dance floor, trailing her long sash behind her. A bouquet of roses spills across her shoulders with the same grace as the stone houses on the hillside in Molise.

Unused to walking in a floor-length dress, Miss Ripabottoni manages the briefest of smiles. She does not bear her responsibilities lightly.

She'd better not.

MY OLD MAN

My old man died on the second of June, of a cancer so muscular and aggressive that it seemed to lift him up and throw him down a dozen times a day, as if he were made of rags instead of flesh and blood.

There were hot spots all over his bones. There was a fist of it near his kidneys, an egg-sized lump under his arm and a great thick slab of it sitting on his chest, above his heart. He tried to fight it off with everything he had. He died with his fists clenched, an inch at a time.

Even though the pain was swift enough to stay one step ahead of the morphine, my old man never admitted there was anything much the matter. As if naming the devil might give it power. When his doctor asked him how he was, he'd reply, "Not so bad," and ask, "How about you?" as if he were making a social call.

He didn't want to frighten anyone with the extent of the disease. He left it to my mother to parse the grammar of his moans at night, so she could tell the doctor what she'd heard when they went together to the clinic in the morning.

My old man was, among other things, a part-time dance-band musician who played spaghetti jobs for nearly sixty years. A spaghetti job is musician's talk in the Lakehead for a dinner dance, even when the food was roast beef and cabbage rolls, and the dance was at the Finn, and not the Italian Hall.

He was a handsome bugger with a banjo on his knee. He was a young man with a slide trombone. Later in life, he leaned against his bass fiddle and caressed it while he sang the blues, and couples on the dance floor held each other close and made love listening to his voice.

I made the mistake one night of taking a date to watch him play. She spent the evening with her elbows propped on the table, her chin resting in her hands, a dreamy expression on her face, staring at my old man, watching him work the slide of the horn sweetly back and forth. Too Freudian, even for me. I took her home and said goodnight and shook her hand.

I spent the last month with my old man, sleeping in an armchair in his hospital room, listening to him gasp for breath at night.

The first week, he was well enough to tell me stories, although he'd often fall asleep before he finished what he was saying. Not that it mattered. He always told the same stories the same way every time he told them. I know most of them by heart. The time he stole the piano. The dog who followed him home. The time his cousin got drunk and fell asleep and let the still blow up.

One night, my old man opened his eyes and lifted his head and looked at me and asked, "Who brought the charges?" I asked him what he meant. He looked away. He said, "There had to have been charges." He thought he was in jail.

The next night, he woke and looked at me again. He said "They can't keep my shoes from me, can they?" He thought if he could get his shoes, he could sneak out. No such luck, Pops.

The second week, the questions tapered off and something happened to the stories. He'd get stuck on certain sentences and repeat them until he forgot what he was talking about. Repeat them until he forgot what he was talking about.

As if his needle was stuck in the groove.

My old man was a small-town Fellini who brought a little magic and a little cruelty to nearly everything he did. One night, when I was a kid and he was playing in the circus band, he brought Victor Julian home for supper. Victor Julian was the guy with the dancing dogs. Victor Julian took one look at my little Trixie, she with the patch over her eye and her little dog grin and her whippet's tail.

Victor Julian smiled possessively.

He waited until I went outside after supper, and then he made my dad an offer. A week's wages, at a time when my folks had no money to speak of, and four boys to raise.

When I came in from playing after supper, the room fell silent. Nobody looked at me. My old man told me Trixie would have a good home with all the other circus dogs. She'd get to travel and see the country. Victor Julian said he'd take her with him on the Ed Sullivan Show.

I was ten years old. It hurt me to see Trixie go. I could understand about the money. We were always broke. But I thought the Ed Sullivan business was a bit much. I thought they didn't have to lie.

Trixie grinned over her shoulder at me as she trotted out the door with Victor Julian. The next day, the newspaper carried a photo of my dog, and a story with the headline "Local Pooch Makes Good."

Six months later, we got a note telling us Trixie was going to be on TV. I didn't want to believe it, in case it wasn't true. I held my breath until Sunday.

During the second half of the show, Ed Sullivan introduced Victor Julian. He stepped on stage in his tux, with his top hat on his head. Following behind him, last in a line of dancing dogs, dressed in a little skirt, with a little hat on her head and a ruffled collar round her neck, grinning ear to ear and wagging her skinny whip of a tail, was my little Trixie.

She jumped through a hoop. She walked up a ladder. She grinned at the other dogs. I forgave my old man instantly. We were still broke, the money was long gone to pay bills, but one of us, even if it was only the dog, had made it to a better life.

Not all of what my old man did ended with a magic turn. In the end, there were too many late nights and too many pieces of himself tendered easily to strangers.

It couldn't have been easy to sell my dog. I forgave him, anyway. He worked hard, he loved his sons, and if he promised us more than he could reasonably deliver, in the end he gave us all he had.

The final week of his life, my old man was down to single words, then gestures. The last thing I saw him do, at quarter to nine on the morning of the last day of his life, was raise his fist and shake it.

Printed in November 1996 by

VEILLEUX
ON DEMAND PRINTING INC.

in Boucherville, Quebec